ADVANCE PRAISE FOR *QUEERING THE TAROT*

"*Queering The Tarot* is an indispensable book in the modern re-workings of the 600-year-old images, symbols, and stories—indispensable, not just for LGBTQQIPA2P+ people, but for anyone who wants to see how the tarot can expand and open to the world. For most of those 600 years, the images represented a hierarchical society assumed to consist of cisgendered, hetero-sexual white people, primarily of the privileged classes. People outside that 'normality' (a Dutch slogan from the 1980's: 'Ever meet a normal person? And did you like it?') learned to subtly code themselves into the pictures. But they didn't see themselves. Now we have a book that joyously embraces all those hidden people, using the cards not just to tackle queer issues but to celebrate who we all are. Is it only for queer people, then? Absolutely not. For 'straight' people, it will not only show them how the rest of the world lives—and how to read for queer people—but what may be most valuable, it will give them the experience of discovering themselves in a set of images and symbols not directly about them."

—Rachel Pollack, author of *Seventy-Eight Degrees of Wisdom*

"*Queering the Tarot* takes the tarot cards that we all love and peels them back to their bones. From there, Cassandra Snow builds the cards anew, in a way that speaks to everyone regardless of their gender identity, sexuality, or gender expression. I have seen queer tarot cards save people's lives. I have seen the impact that diversity and representation have in my community. I am delighted that this book exists, and encourage everyone—queer, straight, or otherwise—to pick it up."

—Melissa Cynova, author of *Kitchen Table Tarot*

"In *Queering the Tarot*, Cassandra Snow opens the world of tarot and makes it inclusive for the LGBTQ+ community and other marginalized folk. I think this may be one of the most important tarot books published in recent years. It gives

much-needed representation and respect to a whole slice of the population that has been left out due to tarot's tendency to focus on white, cisgender, heteronormative. *Queering the Tarot* is a wonderful book whose time has come. It belongs on every serious tarot reader's shelf."

—Theresa Reed, author of *The Tarot Coloring Book* and coauthor of *Tarot for Troubled Times*

"*Queering the Tarot* doesn't just bring the tarot out of the closet. It dresses it up in drag (both queen and king) to show it off. This is a book that isn't afraid to challenge the binary gender paradigm from all angles. It doesn't matter if you are queer, straight, or somewhere else on the spectrum because Cassandra Snow unflinchingly casts aside the heteronormative dialogue to reveal a rich, nuanced view of this divinatory art. I was pleased to see the Urban Tarot used in the images as well. It is the perfect 'gender-queer' deck for this book. It is truly a keeper for anyone who wishes to broaden their tarot practice personally. I think it should be required for all professionals who want to be in touch and in tune with our diverse, beautiful population."

—Arwen Lynch-Poe, editor and publisher at *The Cartomancer* magazine

"Learning to apply the wisdom embedded in each tarot card to specific situations is always a challenge. The challenge is heightened when your lifestyle may not be considered mainstream. Cassandra Snow leads us on a journey through the tarot that explores, acknowledges, and honors the experiences of non-straight and/or noncisgendered folks. Her insights are valuable for both queer readers and for readers with queer clients."

—Barbara Moore, author of *The Steampunk Tarot, Llewellyn's Classic Tarot, Your Tarot Your Way,* and the founder of *www.tarotshaman.com*

QUEERING
THE TAROT

QUEERING THE TAROT

CASSANDRA SNOW

Foreword by Beth Maiden

WEISER
BOOKS

This edition first published in 2019 by Weiser Books, an imprint of
Red Wheel/Weiser, ʟʟᴄ
With offices at:
65 Parker Street, Suite 7
Newburyport, MA 01950
www.redwheelweiser.com

ISBN: 978-1-57863-648-8
Library of Congress Cataloging-in-Publication Data available upon request

Printed in Canada
MAR
10 9 8 7 6 5 4 3 2 1

To all the LGBTQ+ trailblazers to whom I owe everything,
including Genesis Moss (the first lesbian I ever saw on TV),
but especially the Sylvia Riveras, the Marsha P. Johnsons,
and the Harvey Milks of the world.
Thank you for making a better world for all of us,
and I dedicate Queering the Tarot *to you.*

CONTENTS

2

THE SUIT OF WANDS, 71

3

THE SUIT OF SWORDS, 93

4

THE SUIT OF PENTACLES, 115

5

THE SUIT OF CUPS, 139

6

THE COURT CARDS, 159

FOREWORD

Beth Maiden, July 2018

When I look at the surprisingly few, yet dearly loved books on the shelves of my tarot room, I am greeted warmly by queer family and friends. From the veteran Rachel Pollack's classic *Seventy-Eight Degrees of Wisdom* to Michelle Tea's fresh and impassioned *Modern Tarot*, from Barbara Moore's many and wide-ranging tarot guidebooks to the transgenerational project that is *She Is Sitting in the Night* by Rima Athar, Oliver Pickle, and Ruth West, LGBTQ+ folks are all over the tarotsphere, and this makes my queer heart sing.

That's not to mention the queer-centered decks that have recently exploded my once modest collection—*The Numinous Tarot*, the *Shrine of the Black Medusa Tarot*, the Malakh Halevanah deck, the *Delta Enduring Tarot,* and the *Next World Tarot* to name just a few—all the work of LGBTQ-identified creators who have found that tarot, with its infinite capacity for reframing, reinterpretation, retelling, is a perfect medium for sharing and exploring queer stories and experiences.

Whether comfortably taking up space in the mainstream conversation or fiercely reclaiming tarot to reflect the experience of marginalization, seizing the 78 cards we know as tarot and using them to reflect our experiences has become part of our community's lineage and literary canon. Through rereading and retelling the journeys found in the tarot, we explore our collective story, its struggles, its resilience, its growth. A deck of tarot cards in the hands of a young queer is every bit as important and vital as an esteemed text in the queer canon—each and every time the deck is picked up and we lay out those familiar cards, it becomes a new story, its well-known symbols and archetypes ready to be reshaped to reflect our many and diverse lived realities.

• • •

Why is it that queer folks are so drawn to tarot and other witchy, magical, or esoteric practices? I believe it has to do with a righteous reclaiming of the marginal spaces we inhabit. As we embrace what makes us different, we turn to tools and practices that have themselves been ridiculed or shamed. I spoke about the value of queer magic recently in an interview with queer designer and moon-witch Sarah Gottesdiener:

> Queers—especially those with other intersecting marginal identities—tend to exist in the spaces the mainstream neglects: beautiful, scruffy, overgrown edgelands where we can experience a little freedom, support each other to thrive, get real about our pain, and continually look outward. We have to look outward because as well as being reviled and scapegoated, queers are also exotified and tokenized, and the radical spaces we create are rapidly gentrified and commodified, claimed by the mainstream, and sold back to us in plastic packaging. This is always painful, but I think queer folks are used to it. It can be fuel for the fire. We push boundaries and move a little further out of the mainstream, where we discover new sources of inspiration, create new kinds of magic.
>
> We work to liberate ourselves and each other. Queers understand that personal and collective liberation are interwoven and we are used to supporting and uplifting each other in a way that runs counter to the me me me messages of the mainstream. We critique what we are offered (or sold) and turn it on its head.*

To a world that categorizes us as nonnormative, we say, "Your loss! We'll build our own communities, economies, and structures of care right over here." Picking up affordable, accessible practices like tarot, astrology, and herbalism—folk tools that to the capitalist white heteropatriarchy are useless because they can't be neatly explained, co-opted, and sold—is part of this radical community-building process. We use tarot to better understand and care for ourselves and our communities.

Queering the Tarot is a brilliant contribution to this collective work. Cassandra's interpretations zoom in on the generally accepted meanings of each card, examining timeworn archetypes, symbols, tropes, and rites of passage via one simple yet crucial question:

---

* Interview on Sarah Gottesdiener's website, Visual Magic, 2017 https://visualmagic.info/portfolio/beth-maiden-interview/

How can this card relate differently for queer-identified readers?

The asking is itself a radical act. It is a question that makes space for difference. It is a question that centers the marginal, the unseen, and makes it visible.

Too often, mainstream discourse on LGBTQ+ experiences focuses on how queers are "just like everyone else." We hear about "same love," we talk about how we are all human, we fight for permission to enter the patriarchal, capitalist institution of matrimony, and so on. I frequently hear confused voices drifting over from the mainstream, asking: Why do you need your own special hairdressers? Do you still need Pride, now that gays can get married? Why would you seek out a queer therapist? and so on.

These questions contain their own answers; their very asking shows us why and how much we do need these things. While, of course, it's important to talk about human commonalities, while, of course, love is love, and while for many LGBTQ+ people, a seat at the mainstream table is a revolution in itself, it's also the case that the queer experience is different from the hetero experience (depending on other intersecting circumstances such as race, class, mental health, or body type, often vastly so). We need our own hairdressers, visibility parades, therapists, and so on because so often the people and institutions around us *do not get it* (or choose not to). Heteronormative society doesn't know what it is like to have a stylist alter that haircut you've asked for in order to make your gender expression fit their comfort zone, doesn't know how it feels to be continually assessing the fluctuating cost of speaking in your own voice, wearing the clothes you choose, or simply touching your lover's hand. Heteronormative society doesn't see the shame and the fear every queer person has confronted (or will at some point need to confront) that is the result of growing up categorized as not "normal." No single queer person I know (regardless of how supportive their family may be) has been immune to this shame and fear. Queer identity—with all of this shame and fear, and with its pride and its resilience and its deep, unconditional love, too—is a maze through which we walk, or crawl, or fly, or drag ourselves, or dance, or dream, or fall, or fuck, as we journey toward the truth of who we are and who we can be. Tarot is a compass for navigating that maze with curiosity, consciousness, honesty, and compassion.

For any tarot reader, The Fool's Journey is a quest for self-discovery, connection, integration, and healing, culminating in self-actualization, where the individual comes to recognize their unique yet interdependent place in what the poet Mary Oliver beautifully names "the family of things."* For me, endlessly shuffling, endlessly rereading, tarot is the best of tools, because it holds space for everybody and everything in the cosmos. The most common thing I hear from my own tarot clients runs along the lines of "wow—it was so good to get that confirmation." The cards so often tell us what we already know! Over the years, I've come to realize that this is tarot's most beautiful gift. For queer folks—and for anyone experiencing systemic oppression and the layers of fear and shame that come with that—tarot holds up a mirror to the truths we hide away, helping us to piece together our identities and understand the beauty and complexity of our non-normative lives and, ultimately, live them with pride.

Cassandra draws on many years of practice working as a healer, witch, tarot reader, and in other roles at the heart of their LGBTQ+ community, as evidenced by the wide-ranging suggestions offered for each card. In *Queering the Tarot*, the Two of Pentacles speaks of the pride and pain of juggling intersecting identities ("As soon as we gain a cool piece of legislation, we lose another one we were counting on"), The Hermit can open up a conversation around asexuality or aromanticism, and the entire suit of Swords makes space for acknowledging that LGBTQ+ folks are far more likely than their straight peers to suffer with mental health and addiction issues.

Death is another simple example, with its well-understood connotations of transformation and letting go. The difference between reading platitudes around "big life changes" versus on-point notes on, for example, gender transition and deadnames, is massive, and vitally important to a person about to undergo such a change. So, too, is the opening of space to talk about how and why Death's unstoppable change may be happening; when reading about the Death card we often hear that change is inevitable, and it's up to us to embrace it, to go with the flow. A queer-centered reading might also dig into who or what is forcing those changes, since, for example, queer people are so frequently outed before they are ready or before it is safe. Again, the queer experience is witnessed in its complexity and in the context of a heteronormative world, rather than watered down to blend with more normative tarot card interpretations.

** From "Wild Geese," by Mary Oliver, 2004

• • •

These are just a few quick examples. Each on its own can mean that a queer person feels better understood. Together, as a guidebook to the entire tarot, they are a compass, a friendly guide, and a witness to each and every queer journey.

At the same time, there is so much more to explore here. *Queering the Tarot* is one volume. As one author, one reader, one healer, Cassandra can cover only so much ground as they present their interpretations of the cards. I know that Cassandra would be the first to say that this book is a contribution to a huge and ever shifting conversation—not a conclusion or a definitive guide. What is so radical and so wonderful about this book is that it carves out space for that conversation, while its mainstream publication amplifies it, spreads it, opens it further. But don't forget that this conversation is already taking place. It's happening in blogs and in bars, in bedrooms and coffee shops, in parks and on social media. Each time you pick up your deck, you add to the conversation. As you open this book and shift your gaze to take in the perspectives presented here, understand that the cards are a springboard for your own interpretations, prompts for your own self-enquiry. What happens next, what you find in the cards you lay before yourself, depends on you. Will you claim your story—in all of its complexity? I hope so—because that is queer self-love in action, and that is where the revolution happens.

You are witnessed. You are seen. You matter. You belong.

With deep and endless love
for your unique and magical queer journey,
—Beth

WORD

In this book I use the acronym LGBTQQIP2SA+, which stands for Lesbian, Gay, Bisexual, Transgender, Queer, Questioning, Intersex, Pansexual, Two-Spirit, Asexual, and anyone else who identifies as *not straight, not cisgender,* or both. The + is divisive, and I do recognize that not everyone likes their inclusion seeming like an afterthought. I see you, I hear you, and I'm always looking for more inclusive solutions. Please know that I consider anyone who is not both straight and cisgender a Q, as in *Queer.* You're already under the umbrella and celebrating our queerness with us in my eyes.

I also know that the word *Queer* isn't comfortable or right for everyone. This is a word that originally just meant *odd* (another label I happily claim) but, over time, became a slur lobbed at those who were—or were perceived as—something other than straight, cisgender, or both. It was a word meant to hurt us and other us. It was a word used to make us feel that we were different, not welcome, not safe. Over the past several years, our community has done some brilliant work reclaiming this word that once put us in a limiting box. It is now a word that means *out of the box.* It's a word that allows us to take pride in being original, nonconforming, unique, expansive, freeing—all beautiful, wonderful qualities. It has also become a word intended to create community with as many identities and *others* as possible, as we've reclaimed them. The world might think you're different—and maybe they're right. But we celebrate that here in our community, and we welcome you with open arms.

In this book, I embrace polyamory in relationships and families. I myself am genderfluid and certainly welcome genderqueer, gender nonconforming, agender, pangender, and otherwise nonbinary readers. You will see a lot of the singular *they* pronoun as a result. It is not a typo. I embrace elements of relationship anarchism even though I never quite describe it as that. My own queerplatonic partner is the most significant person in my life, even though we do both date and have sex (just not with each other), and the idea that all types of healing and loving relationships can be equally important comes through throughout the book. I also identify with the kink community and am incredibly sex-positive. So sex comes up. A lot. While each of these things could be its own book, I try to delve into them with some gusto throughout this one, among the other marginalized identities and relationships you expect to see.

Queering something, then, means taking what our society has given us and finding our own way, outside of that society's limits. They put us in a box, and we still find ways to create and prosper and make it the most well decorated box you'll see. Queering erases the narrowness and small-mindedness of *normal*. It embraces the beauty, the mystery, and the vastness of our differences. It welcomes everyone who needs a safer space, and it takes responsibility for helping those people heal. Tarot is supposed to help people heal, after all. Yet this stunning divination form does create some division where it means to be welcoming with its binary court cards and stress on values we may not all share. In *Queering the Tarot,* I am literally taking tarot *out of the box.* All genders, sexual identities, relationship orientations, and faiths are welcome at this tarot table—and I sure am glad you found your way here.

WHAT IS QUEERING THE TAROT?

Tarot is a tool of self-discovery, healing, growth, empowerment, and liberation. Tarot archetypes provide the reader with a window into present circumstances and future potential. It is a window that shows us where we've been and where we are going. But what if that window opened up only on a world that was white, European, and heterosexual? The many excellent books that have come to us through the ages focus largely on the symbolism of the cards, and so the interpretations of the tarot that have been passed down through tradition generally presuppose a commonality and normalcy among humanity. But humanity is diverse—culturally, spiritually, sexually. Tarot has the power to serve a greater population if we allow ourselves to unlock the tarot's deeper meanings, if we allow ourselves to *queer* the tarot.

People regularly ask, "Why tarot?" when I tell them what I do with my life. I never even know where to start answering that question because the real answer is that tarot saved my life at a time when I was experiencing a crisis of faith and complete personal meltdown. I was a freshman in college, away from an alcoholic, poverty-laden home for the first time. It was supposed to be a fresh start, but I was raped twice in one month and then lived with a genuine sociopath who stole my identity in a number of terrifying ways while pretending to be my best friend in the world. I was also deeply in the closet, trying to make it work with men and fit into Christian boxes I was never meant to fit into. I was deeply depressed and in the thrall of undiagnosed PTSD. I was lost. I wanted answers from somewhere, anywhere, and when a friend handed me a novelty deck in the basement of our dorm almost as a joke, I started finding them. To me, then, tarot is about healing, survival, and empowerment. It is about finding a way to thrive when the whole world seems to be against you. Tarot is about finding a way through your past and making sure you're not repeating your own unhealthy cycles. Tarot is life. I know that sounds dramatic, but the world is cruel and we need answers, straight talk, and empowerment. That's what tarot gives us, and for many people it's the difference between turning your life around and spiraling into complete disconnection.

Tarot is and can be a tool of the oppressed. It has been by my side as I created a company for queer art and artists, as I developed resources for projects aimed at donating money to Black Lives Matter, and as I encouraged and empowered others to march to the beat of their own drum—and when that drum was taken away, just to march. Yet this set of 78 cards isn't perfect. A standard deck gives in to outdated stereotypes of gender roles, heterosexism, European centrism, and gender binarism. It pushes forward toxic capitalism in much of its approach. It weirdly subscribes to a number of Christian principles, many of which are harmful to almost everyone likely to pick up a tarot deck. If you don't fit into a straight, white, cisgender mold, a traditional tarot deck may not hold much for you. And honestly? Most of us don't fit into that mold. So our tarot practice needs to be as diverse as we are.

In *Queering the Tarot,* I take these traditional ideas and remix them into something relatable and significant for people who are not straight and cisgender. Queering anything is about reclaiming it, making it your own, and subverting it to fit comfortably in your community. I queer theatre in my *other* life by my compassionate and collaborative approach in a field that insists on hierarchies. I queer tarot similarly. I approach the cards from my own point of view—that is, the point of view of a chronically ill, disabled, multiple trauma survivor who is also incredibly queer. I approach the cards from the point of view of someone who wants to liberate the marginalized and works hard to help make that happen. I also approach the cards from the point of view of someone who cares deeply and passionately about the tarot, but whose humanity is the most important thing to them. I boast on my website that all are welcome at my tarot table. I want to show you stories, ideas, and interpretations of the cards that also help you feel welcome at your own.

• • •

I started developing *Queering the Tarot* in a series of articles for TheColu.mn and Little Red Tarot, two amazing websites that have provided a voice and an outlet for me and countless others. My original intention was to explore the tarot from a queer perspective but very early on it became something else entirely: it became a series of questions for and from the cards. Some of these questions were to be expected. For

4

example, the first questions were obviously about gender roles and sexual identity. There is no defined Empress or Emperor in a same-sex relationship, so what are we to make of these traditional female and male archetypes? Over time, though, my exploration of the tarot became about healing from personal and collective trauma. It became about empowerment. It became about creating change and setting fire to the oppression that has kept witches, psychics, people of color, women, and, of course, queer people down for so long. It became about everyone I knew and all of the things they were fighting, and it became about finding ways for us to win.

Queering the Tarot is a book about reclamation. Reading cards has always belonged to the most oppressed, from the extremely persecuted Romani people to modern-day readers from all walks of life. Yet, even now, you will be hard pressed to find any people of color, queer people, disabled people, or people who don't look wealthy in a traditional tarot deck. I wrote this book for all of the people not represented in the aforementioned history of books on the tarot. This book is my love song to my community and to everyone who's been hurt or told they are less than for who they are, whom they love, or where they're from.

Queering the Tarot is a culmination of years of my life's work making the tarot relatable and accessible to LGBTQQIP2SA+ people, including and especially the most marginalized among us. *Queering the Tarot* fights heteronormativity, cisnormativity, patriarchy, and white supremacy. *Queering the Tarot* embraces all body types, all ages, and all generations, loves transgender tarot fans, and believes that bisexuality, pansexuality, and asexuality are every bit as valid as being gay or straight. *Queering the Tarot* is a reclamation of fortune-telling and psychic vision and a deconstruction of the institutions so many hold so dear, but that like to keep anyone *different* from thriving and succeeding. That includes the structure and the traditions inherent in tarot.

Do you need to identify as queer to get the most from this book? No. Although it's tremendously important for me to address the needs of the overlooked LGBTQQ-IP2SA+ community, this book is for any unique soul who has felt wronged, left out, marginalized, different. Which is most people. This book is meant to guide you as you learn tarot, but it's primarily meant to make you ask questions, encourage you to sit with your cards, and learn to let the deck speak to the beautiful, powerful, hurt, confused *you* that you are. *Queering the Tarot* will help you tear down walls, including the ones that block your ability to connect with your deck and to become the super insightful reader I know you can be. In order to enhance your ability to connect with the tarot, I've chosen to illustrate this book with the wonderful *Urban Tarot* by Robin Scott. This deck will visually jump-start your understanding of the tarot in non-normative ways—it is urban, real, contemporary, and it will make you ask questions. And yet, the *Urban Tarot* will resonate with those familiar with the *Rider-Waite-Smith Tarot* deck as well as Crowley's *Thoth Tarot.*

Queering the Tarot can be used with any deck. Use each card's section to get a feel for what the card can and should do or say. Then sit with the card or group of cards for a while. See what personal messages pop up about your life, your subconscious, your community, and your world. It's from there that you can start healing. It's from there that you can begin reading with confidence and joy.

QUEERING
THE
MAJOR ARCANA

1

THE MAJOR ARCANA

Traditionally the Major Arcana are the first twenty-two cards in the deck, ranging from The Fool to The World. (I say traditionally because we are in a bit of a tarot renaissance, and there are so many wonderful decks reinventing what tarot can be.) The cards of the Major Arcana address matters of fate, spirituality, and anything the gods have ordained necessary in our lives. If we consider the suits of the Minor Arcana as representing the four elements of Earth, Air, Fire, and Water, then the cards of Major Arcana indicate the fifth element, Spirit. Spirit assures that we are being guided by higher principles. In truth, I don't stray too far from those accepted assignations—they just look a little bit different. I do believe there are elements of fate at play in our lives, but I don't think we're its pawns. In fact, that's a pretty oppressive viewpoint. The ideas of fate, karma, and one or several gods choosing for us have been used to justify everything from slavery to caste systems to abuse of members in exclusive and dangerous cults. They are no friend to those living in the margins. Yet I am not without a sense of mystery or romance. I do think there are people that are supposed to be in our lives. I believe that there are places we are supposed to visit, things we are supposed to achieve, love we are supposed to know. Does that mean I think we've irrevocably screwed up our lives if we don't? Absolutely not.

To me, then, fate indicates things that are best for us, things where the ball has already started rolling (and are therefore unavoidable), or anything you feel called to do. There are so many places to turn in the Majors for healing, empowerment, or even just to reflect on one's own identity, and that's especially true for queer people. Fate is not necessarily totally divorced from the queer experience, but it's also not the only factor in our ability to heal and thrive. It's important for *anyone* who has been oppressed to be able to take control of their own lives. Autonomy matters to everyone, but it especially matters to people who have spent most of their lives being told they are wrong about who they are and how they feel. We need to claim it, own it, and live it. That makes fate almost a secondary or tertiary factor in our lives. The ball is already rolling on that major career change, for example, but we have other fish to fry while that's picking up steam. So what major role do the Majors play in our lives?

As I've mentioned, these twenty-two cards represent Spirit—the often recognized fifth element. Spirit is our soul, our aura, the *us* that we were given, and the us that we are building. Spirit is what survives and keeps us going in the face of trauma. Spirit is that part of us that is already healed. Spirit is also, of course, the part of us that prays, does magick, and manifests our dreams into reality. The Major Arcana pull together the best of the other four suits. These cards give us the Fire to become powerful activists and fighters. They give us the Water to heal ourselves, and the heart to love in terrible times. They give us the Air to make quick and sound decisions and the logic to ensure we don't float away. And they give us the Earth that allows us to grow and thrive no matter what we are planted in. All of this makes the Major Arcana a powerful series of cards that can be used in any aspect of our lives.

Most often, I use these twenty-two cards to represent the general life and spiritual journeys we are on and where we are in those journeys. Other readers do the same thing, and in fact the Majors are often collectively called The Fool's Journey. When queering the tarot, I take into account the unique ways LGBTQQIP2SA+ people have been hurt and where healing may be needed. I take our unique joys, communities, and chosen families into account, too. I think about what someone's journey specific to *all* of their identities might be, and how each card looks different in that person's journey. Tarot is highly personal, so looking at it as a monolith is always going to get you in trouble. Still, there are points common enough to all of us to explore. With that, let's jump into these cards!

THE FOOL

The Fool promises exciting new beginnings and encourages youthful optimism. This card represents babies being born, college students setting off into the world on their own, and anyone who takes the plunge to ditch their day job and start their own career. It's a card that encourages big, almost fool-ish leaps of faith. Such leaps of faith also require us to keep a positive attitude and assume that things are going to work out for the best. This is true of The Fool more than it is not. It's important to view this card as a card of early stages or starting fresh. There are a lot of cards that show major upheaval, big risks, and new chapters. This one is special because we aren't starting a new chapter. We're starting a totally new book. That means the road ahead might get treacherous, but we're meant to learn from the pitfalls.

The Fool shows up frequently when we're starting on our path toward our soul's purpose. It came up a lot when I made my decision to move to the Midwest. It came up when I started my theatre company. It came up when I said, "screw day jobs," and made writing and tarot my career. All of these were big, bold choices that I knew were right for me. And they were also all times I listened to my intuition and followed what I knew to be a calling. That is really where The Fool shines—in getting us to live out our highest purpose.

It makes sense, then, that this card comes up frequently for queer seekers. (A seeker or querent is anyone turning to the tarot for guidance.) We cannot live our soul's purpose if we are denying pieces of who we are. If you're considering or have recently come out of the closet, you will likely get the encouraging message of The Fool. You really cannot start your soul's journey or work toward your purpose carry-ing big secrets on your shoulders. That's not to say that this card doesn't encourage experimentation. Quite the opposite. Admitting you're queer and deciding which letter of the beautifully long acronym we use now are totally different. My own journey has seen several different identities, all of them queer, and all of them honoring who I truly was at that time.

I mentioned though, that this card came up a lot when I was making my decision to move to the American Midwest. That was an incredibly queer application of this card. Why? Well, I was living in the Bible Belt, attending a Baptist college that refused to let students form a Queer Student Alliance. The college even banned any new groups from being formed on campus in retaliation. I was in the closet for most of that hubbub, and I'm not sure which side of the closet was worse. All I know is that from my side, it hammered home the self-loathing I'd felt over my sexuality for years. It was not a healthy environment for me to be in. The Midwest is hardly a paragon of radical politics, but it's also not a Baptist-run cesspool where even rumors of LGBTQQIP2SA+ students getting together would cause an administrative meltdown. The Fool showed up to encourage me to literally start a new journey, one where I could make my own way and find my own voice in an environment where it was at least marginally safer to do so. That's what The Fool wants for all of us: to find a place where we can truly begin our journey.

The Fool represents *any* time we are starting new or starting over. While the examples I've written about deal with very specific situations that many queer people face in their lifetime, there are countless others. Finding a new group of friends or a queer chosen family is one. Starting a new spiritual journey that won't make you feel crappy for being queer is another. Gender transitions often bring up The Fool. So does that first truly queer relationship (whatever that means to you). Queer applications of The Fool abound in our lives, but its message stays the same: remain true to your identity, trust that inner voice, and jump! Sometimes as LGBTQQIP2SA+ people, that is all the encouragement we need.

THE MAGICIAN

Magick. Luck. Creation. These are just a few key words ascribed to The Magician, a card full of magick and moxie. The Magician represents being able to use the skills and resources at your disposal to create change in your life and the world at large. This card also indicates creating the life you desire through the law of attraction (or other magickal means). This is a next-steps card—The Fool starts us on a journey, and The Magician is what happens once we've traveled for a bit. It's a card signifying that a transformation has happened within, and you are now ready to take all of the skills

and magick contained inside of you out into the world, transforming your own life and creating good for others. The minor prophecies therefore include instances of luck—meetings, emails, phone calls all meant to take our life from the "I'm ready" to the "I'm actually doing this" stage.

When we look at reading for the queer crowd, the base interpretation of this card doesn't change. This is one of those cards where knowing a lot about the queer experience comes in handier than knowing a lot about the tarot. Queer people often go through quite a journey to reach the point of realizing they are a queer person, let alone coming out and living as one, and it can come with a lot of shame and missteps along the way. While The Magician is usually seen as an early-stages life card, for queer people, assuming this would be a mistake. It often takes years to feel comfortable presenting as a gender you weren't assigned at birth. It can take many sexual partners to figure out how you fall in terms of sexual identity, and that goes double for those of us who are kinky too. This card showing up for a queer person is not necessarily about that moment after The Fool, when you realize it's okay to be you. It's possibly years later when you've actually hammered out what *being you* looks and feels like. This, for LGBTQQIP2SA+ people, is when the magick starts happening.

Then, there's the issue of confidence for queer seekers in all other areas of their life. Most marginalized people take years learning the skills they want to build their career from, where others take mere months. Does that mean we're not ready sooner? No. What it means is that our inner voice has been so beaten down (by ourselves or others) that we don't think we can acquire that set of skills quickly enough. We wait to start our lives until we are 1,000 percent sure we know what we're doing. The Magician shows up to encourage us to step out and try for success sooner. This card that brings luck to people who are both straight and cisgender also brings confidence to queer people. That's really important, and a side of The Magician that's easy to miss. We can *all* create the lives we want with spiritual prowess, luck, and the work required. It takes a card as sure of itself as The Magician to make queer seekers see that.

The Magician is a card of literal magick. What that meant for me several years ago while I was still stuck in the Bible Belt was that it was time to explore alternative spiritualities. Christianity in the right hands is every bit as healing and empowering as any other spiritual path. It's not for everybody, though, and a significant number of LGBTQQIP2SA+ people have been hurt by or even pushed out of their home churches because of who they are. Sometimes, what we need to heal that betrayal is a different spirituality altogether. I found witchcraft, ghosts, and tarot in dorm room basements and on various walking paths in the mountains of North Carolina. I was scared at first. I was convinced I was wrong. Some gentle nudging from the tarot and Pagans I trusted eventually won me over, but The Magician showed up a lot for me back then. For all of the life purpose and practical application we see, sometimes this card just wants us to find ourselves spiritually.

THE HIGH PRIESTESS

The High Priestess digs deep, y'all. This is a card of mystery and intrigue, but it's also a card of deep, profound knowledge. This can be a frustrating card to pull at times since we are taking to the tarot to solve mysteries or rely on wisdom that is not our own, but it is often a necessary wake-up call to tune in to ourselves. This card, generally speaking, shows up in one of two ways. Sometimes The High Priestess shows up because we aren't supposed to know what's around the corner. We are new to our path and should still be surprised and excited by the things our Higher Power throws at us. In other

words, it's best not to know. Alternatively, this card comes when all of the answers we need are sitting buried in our guts, our minds, or our bones. There are truths we can see or know, but there are also truths we can feel. The latter are the deepest truths there are, and the ones The High Priestess urges you to seek.

Feeling our truths as queer people is one of the most important gifts we can give ourselves. Where does our awareness of our own queerness start? Our minds? Our hearts? Or somewhere deeper, hidden even to us? We've already seen in our short journey to The High Priestess that LGBTQQIP2SA+ are quieted and have their intuition thrown off by pressure and bigotry from the world at large. This card is a deep, necessary wake-up call to find that voice again.

The High Priestess is all about feeling our truth, and there are few, if any, things more awakening than sex. Queering the tarot, or taking any radical approach to it, means embracing sex positivity and not quieting the significant role it has in most of our lives. The High Priestess is a fairly dominant force, insisting that if they sleep with you, their needs *will* be met. Once a partner enthusiastically consents to these conditions, though, game on. Queering The High Priestess means committing to your own pleasure, indulging in sensuality, and finding partners who genuinely enjoy being under you. Don't settle for less than that; you've been through enough in your queer life.

As we talk about The High Priestess' enviable sex life, we touch on another important message for queer seekers: don't settle for less than what you deserve—ever. It is heartbreakingly common for me to see my community members take jobs that do not pay enough because they are queer friendly, or, alternatively, take jobs where they must stay somewhat closeted because they need the money or benefits offered. There's not always a positive solution to this. Sometimes we have to balance the harsh reality queer people live in with our own needs. When The High Priestess is on the table though, that simply isn't true. You can have a partner who stokes your intellectual fires *and* accepts your gender identity. You can have a job that is lucrative *and* safe. You can be who you are *and* meet your needs. Don't worry about the details for now. This card loves its mysteries. It will all sort out the way you need it to, though, only so long as you refuse to settle for less than what you know in your bones you deserve.

THE EMPRESS AND THE EMPEROR

As we continue to journey through the tarot, queering it every step of the way, some cards make more sense to queer as a set or a series. The Empress and The Emperor are two such cards. Traditionally these cards are seen as *Mother* and *Father,* each representing the best and worst of those archetypes. The Empress is historically said to deal with maternal energy. This is understood to be the nurturing side of ourselves, as well as the side that deals with unconditional love. She's also a positive omen for creative energy and fertility. In the negative, this card can represent a flare-up of mommy issues, or love that is overbearing. Not very flattering, but The Emperor has a dark side, too. This card represents so-called fatherly wisdom and the self-discipline we supposedly all learned from our dads. The card also represents control and stability, and, sure enough, angry or strict fathers are also represented here.

Most readers, at least at the professional level, have figured out how to read around gender in the court cards, but this pair presents a different challenge. Mother and Father are different archetypes with deeper ingrained biases than King or Queen, or even Male or Female. To truly queer these two, you have to be willing to throw out any gendered notions of them—not only to acknowledge same-sex relationships, but also to acknowledge the experience of transgender people, including those who don't identify on the binary. Furthermore, the way these cards interpret Mother and Father is troublingly outdated in a world where dads often stay home and do the nurturing, moms are frequently charged with both roles, and many people aren't even raised by their birth parents.

The Empress, boiled down to the card's core, represents nurturing and creative energy. This is often a person with lots of love to give. This describes as many men and genderqueer people in my life as it does women. I would actually argue that since I run in primarily queer circles, this is more likely than not to represent a non-female friend when it shows up for me. While there are a lot of negative stereotypes of feminized gay men, they do exist, and you know what? They are strong, beautiful, and radical. They also serve as moms to young queers of all ilks who are still in or struggling to come out of the closet. Like The Empress, their love can also be a little bit clingy and overbearing sometimes. As traits, these are not inherently negative, though. They just want to make sure you're okay! Regardless of gender, The Empress brings so much of the heart to the queer community. Queering this card is not just accepting that all genders can be The Empress. The Empress queered is gay or queer bars that are inclusive. The Empress queered is queer open mic nights where anything goes. The Empress queered is letting friends crash on your couch because they have nowhere else to go, buying your friend who doesn't have a job a coffee to perk them up, handing down your old clothes to someone who's transitioning.

The Empress is also art and creativity. She is, then, any space where queer art thrives or people are creating from their souls. In this concept of creativity, we break down that word and get *create*. This card shows up when we can have any future we want, and it's time for us to set that into motion. Growing up, I was told "college, husband, good-paying job, kids"—in that order. Sometimes people actually said this to me, but much of it was subliminal. The Empress showed up when I rebelled slightly by choosing to major in theatre. She showed up big time when I had to figure out what I was doing in Iowa with a theatre degree and a backpack full of spellbooks. The world was my oyster then, and I could see that. I just needed to spend some time visualizing what I was supposed to make out of all this.

While it may be clear that I'm a pretty big fan of a big queered-up Empress, The Emperor is harder for me—to say the least. The Emperor in his simplest form is about control and stability, and those are not bad traits. However, the art and the undertone of this card are often so harsh that it seems the message that comes through most often is control and stability at any cost. This is a hella dangerous concept for anyone, but especially for queer people whose rights are constantly being given and taken away by our governments and dangled like bait as options for "compromise."

Very few tarot cards, however, are strictly good or bad. The Emperor may show up to say, "Hey, uh, someone really does have a lot of control over you right now. Sorry," or, "Yeah, no, that's going to happen because of this patriarchal law in place." Frequently, though, he shows up to tell us the exact opposite thing, and that's pretty great. This means, in a reading The Emperor is often telling you to take back control of your life. This card showed up before I started trauma therapy. It also showed up before I moved out of an apartment that I shared with a roommate who had broken my heart, and whose continued presence prevented me from healing or being productive. That's actually a really *good* sign for LGBTQQIP2SA+ querents. You are being told to take your life back, which means you have the resources and capacity to do so. That's great!

With all of this queering and healing and taking back of control, why do I still hate this card? Well, for starters, I think most of us would agree we'd rather not be bullied into submission in the first place. Even as we move beyond that, though, taking back control is hard. Trauma therapy was awful but necessary. I had to admit a close relationship was over for good when I moved out of that apartment. I also had to find a new apartment and buy a whole bunch of new stuff! It was genuinely awful. Yes, I'm glad I did it. I still wish I hadn't had to. That's maybe a bit of nontraditional wisdom that I do have for queer folk about The Emperor: it's okay to be mad or feel put upon that you're in this position. You didn't do this. The card wants you to regain control of your life, but that doesn't mean you have to enjoy the process.

Alternatively to everything I just wrote about, it is a sad truth that those of us who identify as not straight or not cisgender frequently have strained relationships with our parents. It's also a sad truth that the damage of those relationships can and does prevent us from moving forward in our lives. It is not uncommon, then, for a parent of any gender to be seen as the cruel and dominating Emperor. It's certainly not uncommon for negative associations with the mother in The Empress to come out in a reading for queer people either. There are appropriate times to gender cards. Normally I would say that those times are strictly when doing so is affirming and healing to the seeker. Sometimes though, we really do have to wade through the crap we were born into in order to reach breakthroughs. For many of us, that means taking a hard look at how our relationships with our parents have affected our queer adult psyches and relationships.

THE HIEROPHANT

Full disclosure: I am not a fan of The Hierophant at all. It's not hard to see why. Traditionally, The Hierophant was based on the Pope and represented religious leaders. To me, that indicates a conservative orthodoxy that was popular during Catholic reign. As time passed, church and state have separated in many countries, and The Hierophant has come to represent government and other institutions like college and marriage. The card also indicates tradition. While I personally struggle with most of those things, readings of The Hierophant are not exclusively negative. Some people see a calling in this card to become a teacher, leader, or healer. Some people take it as a sign that we are in good hands with the institutions in our lives. It can be a healing energy or important time of learning for a querent. Some people spin a card of tradition to be about thinking about one's own traditions and what has always worked for them.

Let's get real though. For most queer seekers, their experiences with the institutions of church and government have not been positive. Many have been rejected by churches and are still denied equal rights and dignities by the government. Even with the increase in countries allowing same-sex marriage, institutionalized queerphobia is so deeply entrenched in most cultures that we hear "institution" and it's not a far jump to "systematic oppression." Hate crimes are still underpenalized. In many places you can still lose your job and your home for being a LGBTQQIP2SA+ person. Most places have not even begun to make progress on trans rights and dignities. And that's just for starters. There are countless other ways the religious and government institutions that are supposed to keep us safe dramatically fail us. Most recently I have been frustrated by the way those institutions use us as props. When we are needed to win an election, everything is "gay marriage" this and "trans rights to bathrooms" that. When we become a liability or even a difficulty, though, we are taken off the table and swept under the rug. It's infuriating. It makes The Hierophant really, really hard for me to swallow in any situation.

If you have a negative view of any card, you do not always have to spin the card positively. I spent years doing this with clients and even in the early days of writing this *Queering the Tarot* project. Sometimes this card comes up because you are being backed into a corner by the very institutions that are supposed to protect you. That sucks. You need to know that, though, if you want to move past or move on from it. The card may not offer advice on its own. Rarely will you pull just one card to gain clarity on a situation, so look to surrounding cards for advice. On its own though, it really could go either way. If you're super backed into a corner, it might be time to call it quits and find a different path. However, if surrounding cards indicate breaking things, healing, or starting over, the hurt and bondage of the traditional Hierophant in our lives could be on its way out. Essentially, The Hierophant could mean the opposite of its traditional meaning—that a break and healing from harmful systematic and institutional oppression is possible. If we want to go really big, sometimes The Hierophant even shows up to call you to action that disrupts or tears down the status quo. This card's healing energy *is* powerful, and you may be just the force to fix what's broken in this situation.

Not every queer person hates The Hierophant as much as I do. I mentioned earlier that healing energy is strong in this card. It is. This card then can often be a calling to take up healing others in your spiritual journey, or could be calling you to leadership in your LGBTQQIP2SA+ community. For many, institution means resource, so The Hierophant could be guiding you toward working for or at a trusted resource in your community.

The Hierophant is a big card, even among other Majors, so whether you're being told to set fire to existing institutions, build your own, or simply learn Reiki so you can help queer people individually, the card is guiding you toward a higher purpose. It may not be your soul's purpose or why you are here, but if we're looking at the Major Arcana as an adventure book, The Hierophant is an important side quest that shapes who you are and what your world will look like when this particular chapter concludes.

THE LOVERS

The Lovers card is usually pretty straight-forward. Love, attraction, and raw passion rule when The Lovers kicks off or sits in the middle of your reading. However, this card is more complex than meets the eye. While sex or manifestation is clearly on the table, this is ultimately a card of choice. You have come to a major fork in the road, and you have to choose which way you're headed. It shows up most often for people who have been sitting at the fork entrance, trying to build a life there, but knowing it's in vain. Frequently the dual meanings in this card let querents know that they need to include their partner in their decision-making process. It shows up when people have been in relationships for a while but have yet to commit to the next step. It also shows up when we are manifesting all the right things in our lives but have to decide which path really is our best one.

The most common queer interpretation that I see in The Lovers is with poly-amorous or non-monogamous clients. New relationships or sexual partnerships are almost always on the table, but there are still big decisions to be made about how many relationships is too many and how to balance new partners with existing ones. Don't worry—we do see cards where people live harmonious polyam lives where this constant rebalancing and love math are no longer necessary. We're not quite there with The Lovers, though. Either we haven't gotten our bearings in our relationship structure, or we're still figuring things out. That's okay. The Lovers insists we make a decision, but it doesn't have to be today. Your choices will be in front of you for a while yet, but know that most potential partners won't wait forever without some kind of reassurance.

Something many queer people face that straight and cisgender people definitely do not is the reality of romantic relationships where one party is not ready to be fully out of the closet. It may be legitimately unsafe for them to be so. Nevertheless, we all have our own needs. Sometimes we can be fully head over heels in love with someone but can't imagine keeping our relationship quiet indefinitely. There isn't a right or wrong solution to this problem in the grand scheme of things, but there *is* what's most important to you. The Lovers obviously encourages us to follow our hearts. So if you find yourself in this situation, ask yourself what your heart wants or needs more. Is it this relationship? Is it a fully out relationship? Is there a compromise that can be met? This is your decision to make, but you do need to make it.

As we continue queering this card, we need to look at what we're told about relationships versus what we actually want. A collective unconscious of what relationships are and what they look like does creep into most of our brains when we are being raised in our heteronormative society. Many people—even people who are LGBTQQIP2SA+—may see their relationships progress by following the same path a straight couple likely does. In many cases, the hard choice comes when we think about what we want in lieu of that. We may not ever want to get married, because that seems like a purely society-driven desire. We may choose not to have kids even with the plethora of options available to us. Alternatively, we may decide to because our love is awesome too and we deserve to raise a family if we choose to. Declaring that your family is a family too is still radical. That choice, though, has to come from your and your partner's desire and not because that's what people expect you to do.

Outside of our romantic lives, some of these same quandries exist. If you are head over heels in love with a field, or a spiritual community, or anything else where you'll have to keep quiet about your politics or your identity, The Lovers calls you to weigh all of that out and make the decision your heart needs you to make. It's okay if your mom, your partner, or your friends don't understand. This one is all you, baby, and you've got to follow your own heart.

THE CHARIOT

Someone with a strong will who can overcome obstacles and triumph through anything frequently receives The Chariot in
a reading. This card is a favorite of many
clients of mine because it assures us that,
though the work is hard and the road
fraught, we will ultimately triumph. This
card also shows up when people are having trouble making a major life decision
like going back to grad school or changing careers. The Chariot wants you to take
that leap of faith and go down the path you
most want, no matter what. However, once
you do there is no turning back, and that

can be daunting. The Chariot calls on us to excercise fierce control and determination, but ultimately takes us to our goal. As a fun side note, travel and transportation
are also well aspected with this card.

Sometimes The Chariot shows up fairly early in our journey as queer people,
addressing whether it's time to come out of the closet, begin transitioning, or start
multiple relationships after coming out as polyam. While those roads have many
speed bumps, this card does promise that living as our true selves will ultimately
lead to a far better place in life. About those speed bumps, though—don't ignore
the threat of them. Movies aimed at queer audiences will lead you to believe that
an openly queer life leads to one of two things: utter despair or even death, or a
happy, jolly land of nonstop sex and laughs with our chosen family. In reality, life is
still just life. In some ways it is harder for LGBTQQIP2SA+ people, but I do think that
makes our joyful moments even more joyful. Don't overlook the hardships that may
be coming down the pike for you, but remember, The Chariot also says it's important
to proceed on your journey anyway.

The Chariot appears most often for people with a very strong will. That does
mean that this card very frequently shows up for young dominants who are still

merely fascinated by BDSM relationships. They could be in an early learning stage. They could be someone who didn't realize they were dominant until a partner awoke something in them. For many of us, kink is just for the bedroom and doesn't affect our day-to-day lives, but for others, dominance or submission runs very deep. There are lifestyle submissives and dominants, and a large number of them are LGBTQQ-IP2SA+. It's important to me to include this community when I read. Queerness should be kink inclusive. All of us are just trying to reclaim our bodies and identities in the way that makes the best sense for us. A young or new dominant may be full of confusing and conflicting thoughts and need the guidance of The Chariot to encourage them to keep learning, growing, and, when it's time, practicing their dominance in healthy and safe ways.

The Chariot frequently appears as a "partway through our journey" card. While I did use it as an example above, it's less likely to see someone coming out via The Chariot. It's more about continuing your journey as optimistically as you started it with The Fool. That means The Chariot often shows up during a speed bump. You've been out for a while, and now your family is doubling down on what was previously just casual queerphobia. Or your employer somehow didn't know you were trans until you wore a certain outfit to work, and then all hell broke lose. Or you've been living it up, enjoying a happy, fulfilling sex life with multiple partners but then you fooled around and fell in love. Now your feelings are scaring you. In any of these situations, The Chariot does implore us to keep going. We will get through this speed bump, and it will be glorious when we do.

STRENGTH

Strength is a card that frustrates many readers and querents at times because we want it to be more complicated than it is. Most cards have multiple meanings, or the word signifying the card is only a starting point. This isn't necessarily true of Strength. There are multiple definitions of strength depending on whom you ask, and that accounts for much of the differentiation in this card between decks. This card could show up as a simple call to wield strength through adversity or quarrels. It could pop up as a reminder that you are strong and can get through anything. I most often see the card as a call to find balance between force and gentle compassion. The most common image on a Strength card is a woman taming a lion through physical affection, which is a lot of what strengthens that latter message.

All of the aforementioned interpretations are incredibly and especially relevant to queer seekers, of course. I've discussed a bit about the unique life path and roadblocks queer people face, and so the Strength card is a welcome gesture to us from our Higher Power. This card could, for example, show up when someone is living or working in an unsafe situation where they cannot come out of the closet or live as their true selves. In this instance, Strength would be a reminder that the person can get through this situation. The card assures them that, as difficult as things are, the seeker is only partially through their journey. Things will turn around if they can power through it for now.

Occasionally this card shows up to remind us to stand up for ourselves. If you know your employer won't fire you, you don't have to listen to homophobic jokes in the break room. If you know your doctor will, with some prodding, give you, as a trans person, your HRT, it's okay to poke them a little about that. Standing up for yourself gets harder every time society pushes us around a little, but if Strength is showing up, you're in a good position to exercise your rights.

Strength also frequently shows up for queer people when we are dealing with activist communities to remind us that the change we are fighting for is worth the force and endurance it takes to see it through. When it shows up *a lot* for us as queer activists, we could be called to activist leadership. This card, as mentioned earlier, can indicate striking a balance between force and gentleness. For activists, that could mean assessing your tactics to see if they are working. Sometimes we are being too kind and too polite, and it's time to tear down our capital city's walls. Sometimes though, the powers that be would be more willing to listen if we talked to them like people. Look at your life as an activist when this card comes up. If you're being too gentle, go harder. If you've been going hard, though, it may be time to scale back and try a kinder approach.

Strength as a card is incredibly straightforward, but it is extremely crucial in a queer person's life. Most often it is a call for us to be strong, or reminding us that we *are* strong. As a marginalized group, we have made huge strides in rights and visibility in the past decade, but there is so much more to do. So many people still live in fear or live incredibly oppressed lives. More often than not, Strength comes to affirm our worth and power in this world. The lessons of the Strength card are not complicated to explain—but they are very difficult to internalize and accept. As queer people we are by necessity bottomless fountains of strength. We are fighting a hard battle forward, though, and sometimes we need a reminder of that very Strength we've been relying on all along.

THE HERMIT

The Hermit in most tarot decks lives isolated, usually in nature, relying on the Earth
and an ancient spiritual wisdom that only
they have access to. Interpreting this card,
at least on the surface level, usually sees us
encouraging querents to learn to love their
time alone and to use it for spiritual purposes. Frequently it shows up for newly single people, warning them not to jump into
something else too quickly, and very often
it's a card of self-reliance. Alternate readings
can include maturation and the inner peace
and wisdom that come with aging.

This is a very important card for those of
us who are queer. On the most basic level, those with unaccepting families will find
themselves walking a Hermit's path before falling into a chosen family, and while
this is not exclusive to queer experience, it is all too common in our community. If a
querent's question revolves around how the coming out process will go, The Hermit
serves as both a warning that the conversation may not go ideally, but also as a reassurance that the wisdom and peace needed for dealing with this blow are already
present within oneself. The Hermit showing up at all reminds us that making time to
take care of ourselves is necessary, and that there are always periods of time when
we must rely wholly on ourselves. In a queered reading, this is especially true. Along
these same lines, that first queer breakup, standing up for ourselves to friends or
family that judge but don't disown us, and periods of questioning our gender or
sexual identity may lead us to a time of The Hermit. That is, a period when we must
spend time alone, walking our own path even when it feels lonely. The flip side of
this walk bears amazing news, though. If you take the card's advice, you are not just
looking at gaining a sense of pride and independence. You are looking at a series of
spiritual and emotional breakthroughs, life-changing epiphanies, and a side order of
strength of conviction that you didn't know was possible. This doesn't change for

LGBTQQIP2SA+ querents, but it's a crucial promise of a pot of gold at the end of an otherwise painful period of rainbows that people in our community need more than their straight, cisgender colleagues.

I would, of course, be remiss if I didn't bring up asexuality and aromanticism, particularly if The Hermit shows up repeatedly for a client. When a client asks why they haven't met anyone that excites them, or regularly senses a lack of connection with sexual or romantic partners, The Hermit will likely show up. This can be a tricky topic to broach, and I actually don't recommend flat out asking, "Do you think you might be asexual or aromantic?" Suggesting that not everyone finds their happiness in romantic or sexual relationships, and asking the seeker to consider how important sexual and romantic attachment are to them is a more gentle and compassionate way to handle this, but still gets the point across. I do want to add here that not every asexual person is aromantic and vice-versa, but both may abstain from sexual or romantic relationships for various reasons, including their own desire or lack thereof. This is another reason it's important to broach asexuality tactfully, and it also allows room for the fluidity that other cards may bring later in the seeker's life.

Tarot readers are not sexuality experts or therapists. The job of the tarot cards or a tarot reader is not to label, diagnose, or otherwise decide for the querent—it is to provide them information, inspiration, and empowerment so that they can do these things for themselves. For the purposes of queering the tarot, however, knowing that repeated showings of this card in regards to romantic or sexual questions could connect to an asexual or aromantic identity is vital.

My final note along these lines is an acknowledgment that not everyone who abstains from romantic or sexual relationships is aromantic or asexual. Illness, religious beliefs, trauma, and gender dysphoria could lead someone who is LGBTQQ-IP2SA+ to choose to live a Hermit's life. As mentioned earlier, not labeling the client is incredibly important in these cases, and if any of these reasons are present, their solitude could be fluid or the querent may find themselves willing to move away from The Hermit later on. That in no way changes the present reality, and all of this should be considered carefully when engaging with the querent. Obviously a lot of this compassion and tact can go out the window if you're just reading for yourself, but it's still important to know that repeated showings of The Hermit do not necessarily mean it will remain in your life forever.

The Hermit will show up for everyone at some point in their lives. Solo time is crucial, but what's more crucial is the art of self-reliance and the ability to access the deepest magick and highest spiritual plane within yourself. For queer or questioning people, this time can be life-altering in the best possible way, but it bears noting that we may fall into this time period through less than joyous circumstances. Additionally, readings should be informed and compassionate for people of all identities, and that includes asexual and aromantic querents.

Queering The Hermit should take all of those possibilities into account without judgment or the temptation to label a querent. In any case, the advice of The Hermit is simple, and even simple to queer. Honor one's truest and highest self. Prepare to walk a necessary path even if that means you do it alone. Solitude is important. Even if the solitude lasts a while or forever, that too can be a beautiful gift. Focusing on these points will empower someone and allow them to make the necessary revelations on their own. After all, The Hermit sees us through important epiphanies, so, as readers, knowing when to back off and let the seeker find their own way is just as important as giving surefire step-by-step advice in other cards.

THE WHEEL OF FORTUNE

The Wheel of Fortune goes by many names; you may know it as the Wheel of Time, of Fortune, of the Zodiac, or simply the Wheel, for example. It's a beloved card for people who have been having a rough go of it. It's a card that promises that everything has its season, and often assures you that *your* season is coming. Big changes are due, and while change is always scary, if you adapt quickly, you are headed straight for success. Traditionally, this card is imbued with a lot of arguably feminine energy. Maiden, Mother, and Crone are present to see us through the Wheel of Time and bless us with The Wheel of Fortune. This can be a bit of a problem for those of us interested in queering the tarot, as I try to abolish gender roles and notions of what these roles are expected to do, but in this card these ideas actually serve us well.

The Maiden, Mother, and Crone in the Wheel of Fortune are not visibly partnered. They do not have male counterparts that we see. There is no Knave, Father, Hermit cycle to parallel this in a different card even though certainly these archetypes exist and are important to tarot. This innately puts the all of the power in this card—and there is significant power in this card—into the hands of women. In spite of many of my problems with traditional interpretations, this is actually a really awesome base to work from. This card, in spite of its feminine ascriptions, makes femininity a powerful, life-altering concept and in our heterosexist patriarchal society, that's a beautiful thing. This is the rare card where I will advise people to embrace its femininity. This card shows off many of the wonderful traits attributed to femmes. Adaptability is one such trait, and it reigns in this card as the key to the querent's success. "Learn to adapt," the Wheel of Fortune says. Make the best out of change, and success is yours.

I love all the fierce femme energy in this card for many reasons. We've looked at how powerful and positive that feminine energy can be in this card, but there's a flip side to this card's absence of masculinity. Because we are conditioned to think in binaries, that absence of masculine counterparts allows The Wheel to lend itself to androgyny for those with whom femininity does not resonate. Without male counterparts, established gender roles fall away, and we are left with simply powerful, magickal entities that help us usher in the changes that we need. This card speaks deeply to transfeminine and non-binary querents for this reason, and promises that these sides of themselves can carry them through any major life or spiritual changes they are undergoing.

This brings us nicely into queering what some of those changes are. There are some readings where this card will not need to be queered. The Wheel of Fortune in a career or finance spread is pretty simple: "Congrats, good things are coming." The Wheel of Time in a reading based on a straightforward question about relationships simply tells us, "Yes, the time for this is on its way. It may not be now, but it is coming." Certainly for any marginalized person, that message is even more powerful, affirming, and important. The base message, though, is still the same.

As we look at queerness and identity, though, there are some changes specific to a LGBTQQIP2SA+ person's life that this Wheel could bring. This card, like The High Priestess, can indicate elements of fluidity in one's gender or sexual identity. A fixed identity could start shifting, or a fluid identity could end up stabilizing. For transgender querents looking to take bigger steps in their transition, this card is an excellent sign of opportunity and change headed their way. For those struggling to come out, move into their next big, queer relationship, or jump into activist opportunities, this card is the loving anvil on the head from the universe telling you to go for it. If you're simply looking for such opportunities or relationships, this is a promise that those opportunities are on their way. Furthermore, as politically our society has started moving away from the progress we made over the past previous decade, I often look for The Wheel in readings. I want to know that a total shift of power is coming, preferably a shift that puts that power into the feminine hands we discussed earlier. I can't promise, based on recent readings, that that change is imminent, but the Wheel stands tall, promising that change is inevitable. Something, somewhere has to give eventually—and that's what all queer people need to know right now.

JUSTICE

Justice is usually interpreted pretty much the way you'd expect from a card named Justice. This card is considered to embody balance, fairness, and cause and effect. Justice in this sense is most often described as the universal sense of Justice—good things happen to good people. Like The Hierophant, this card can also indicate matters of the law, government, and societal mores of right and wrong. According to many interpretations, honesty is essential when Justice comes up. Those who are honest, even if they were wrong initially, succeed when this card arises.

It's easy then to queer this card by recognizing that many of the legal systems in place in our society are actually quite oppressive to queer persons, especially transgender people who have to wade through frequently insurmountable red tape to live their lives the way they should be able to. Hate crimes are under-punished across the board, and the law is frequently not on our side in matters of fair housing and employment practices. Most of us who are queer activists are intersectional in our activism, and prison and justice reforms are a huge issue when it comes to the rights and dignities of people of color. These issues, like most things, impact queer people disproportionately and specifically, and that needs to be recognized when we're talking about queering the Justice card.

A queer reading of this card would acknowledge that in spite of universal truths of fairness, the literal mundane law and justice may not be on the querent's side at all, and advice should come based on this information. Often we want to assume that if the querent tows the line, things will work out for them, but, more often than not, that really isn't true for marginalized people. Furthermore, even if karmic justice is on their side, dealing with the legal system could be traumatic for an individual querent. Which means this card, while still aspecting a judgment in their favor, could trigger trauma responses and panic attacks, and that needs to be handled very differently from someone who is dealing with the legal system from a more privileged standpoint.

An alternative but related queering of this card invokes the heart of the card separate from oppressive legal constructs. It evokes what many of us who are queer know to be true—the law and its interpretation aren't always just. Social justice is frequently indicated here for queer clients, and when this card is received, one may be receiving a call to pursue an activist role. True justice does tend to prevail in the long run with the Justice card; fighting for what we know to be right and fair is well aspected here. This card could also be a simple call to balance one's personal and professional life with a more engaged community role. At its core, Justice is also about honesty; if it shows up for a timid or semi-closeted client, it could actually bring good news when this querent speaks their truth.

This is a card that, when queered, makes the surrounding cards incredibly important. A showing of cards indicating bad news or oppressive systems likely warns you of the oppression that legal justice can bring. A showing of Strength or cards indicating communication likely means you should speak your truth no matter what. Things will turn out in your favor. If a querent receives other cards of balance, Justice is a simple reminder to keep all one's balls in the air. Of course, if happy cards or cards of triumph surround Justice, that favorable outcome intended for the Justice card in legal (or other) matters is at hand.

Where things get tricky is when a querent gets both The Hierophant and Justice cards. Both cards can indicate oppressive systems hampering your ultimate destiny—but they can also be calling on you to take on a role where you fight for social justice and become more involved with changing your society's skewed view of justice. The latter is how I most often read this pairing, because I do believe it to be well intentioned in a way that I don't see with other potentially oppressive cards. Maybe it's because I truly believe honesty is the best policy (unless safety issues are at hand), a thought deeply engrained in this card. Maybe it's because I do take on a lot of activist roles and energy in my life. Either way, I personally see the Justice card as pulling us toward a greater, more universal sense of its true definition.

Queering Justice frequently comes down to shucking our notions of law as a construct, and getting back more to a karmic and social sense of justice. There are so many reasons or ways a person could be called to action. The Justice card frequently queers to get us thinking in that vein. Surrounding cards will confirm your sunny view of Justice and The Hierophant or skew you back toward advising a client how to survive or escape an oppressive situation. Justice as a word itself means many different things to many different people—as such, this is arguably one of the more subjective cards in the deck. If reading for yourself, follow your own gut response.

THE HANGED MAN

The Hanged Man is one of my very favorite cards. This surprises a lot of people because, to many, it is card about being being stuck. There is an often uncomfortable need to surrender present, if we are to move out of feeling stuck. The card can be about restriction—sacrificing something you want now for more success further down the line. In contemporary decks especially, The Hanged Man has evolved to indicate letting go, releasing our need for control, and surrendering to our current situation. With The Hanged Man, the surrender leads to both enlightenment and escape from the current entrapment.

Most queer people can recall a time they felt stuck or ensnared because of their queer identity and had to find a way out of the situation. Noting that the querent receiving The Hanged Man is stuck because they are queer, and not stuck through any wrongdoing or misstep on their part, is an important distinction to make. It is likely that at some point an LGBTQQIP2SA+ client has been cornered or silenced when advocating for themselves and their identity in the workplace, to their family, or within a social structure that developed prior to coming out. With The Hanged Man, being stuck means one of two things: either you must cut yourself free under duress—advocating for yourself and your right to speak—and in the process risking who knows how much, or you surrender to the experience, acknowledge that you are stuck and there's not much you can do about it, and accept that there will be unfair, painful times in your life due to not fitting into a heteronormative mold.

Neither option is wrong, and unless the surrounding cards clearly point the reader in one direction or the other, both options should be treated as equally viable and understandable. The Hanged Man teaches hard lessons, one of them being that sometimes life is unfair or hard. So, our choices are laid before us. We can refuse to be stuck and sacrifice whatever is at stake, free ourselves, or surrender to being stuck while trusting that you will wiggle free in due time. Jobs are important. Families are important. These are just two of the many situations that keep us in The Hanged Man position that are likely a big part of the querent's life and shouldn't be dismissed as easy to overcome. Only the querent can decide what the right choice is—but your intuition and surrounding cards should provide further advice.

The Hanged Man has also queered itself in many a reading about activist roles, how to fit being an active member of the queer community into one's overall life, and what to do when you are out and proud and being stifled by a close friend or partner who isn't. Many times in this case, sacrifice is key and leads you to enlightenment and deeper freedom. If you're ready to throw yourself into the fight for trans rights even though it will out you at work, or if you're ready to marry your life partner in spite of your family's objections, or if you are facing a number of social and religious persecutions for making a huge, visible decision, this card will likely show up as a reminder that yes, this is going to suck. You are sacrificing something you care about for something you care even more deeply about. You should still do that. Like all keywords in the tarot, sacrifice is sometimes necessary for a well-rounded, whole life. This isn't easy. The cards see you, feel you, and hear you. You should still do the hard thing. It's not an easy choice, but when we are in love, called to a role in our community, or desperate to live our truth, it is the choice we need to make. Sacrifice in this case, though, does come with a light at the end of the tunnel. You did the right thing. You followed your truest self. You embraced your higher calling. And you can be sure this will provide all you need further down the line.

Then there are times The Hanged Man firmly calls us to surrender to the situation at hand and ride it out until it starts to make sense. Some of these circumstances are much more fun to talk about, and certainly this is one of those cases where queering the tarot makes for a happier interpretation. Traditionally when The Hanged Man calls you to surrender it comes with a whole lot of resistance from the querent, and I don't always see that when queering this card. For example, there is an idea of sexual or romantic fluidity that The Hanged Man sometimes hints at, and for some it can be a major upset in one's thinking and identity when they find themselves attracted to someone they didn't think they could be, or when they start to question their gender roles. However, my experience as a reader has been that when The Hanged Man comes up in this case, the querent has already decided just to ride this out and see what happens. That pain, frustration, and confusion have already been dealt with or didn't factor in. Many LGBTQQIP2SA+ querents feel comfortable surrendering to their own changing tide and hanging out in this new mysterious phase for a bit.

The Hanged Man is also one kinky card. Look at any given set of tarot cards you have, and you'll see this person just happily swinging, all bound up. We've talked about the importance of surrender when it's a sacrifice and how that affects queer seekers, but there's a sexier side of surrender, too. The Hanged Man shows up when we want more in our relationships, but what we want more of might not be clear to us. This card says we want our partner to take control, tying us up and making us beg. We are ready to enjoy being dominated. We feel safe and secure. This partner is, for sure, not going to cut the rope and make us fall. They will leave us there until it's painful and we're a little scared, but mostly, we're thrilled and excited and eager for more. This side of The Hanged Man can be a metaphor . . . but it can also be just what it is.

DEATH

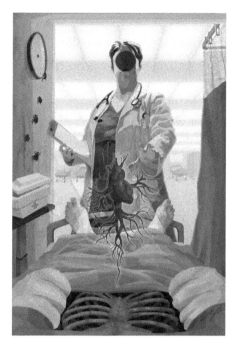

Death gets a bad rap, but everything good that has ever come to me has come after a time of significant and painful endings. Doors close, relationships die, we become totally new people all the time. I get why that's painful and hard for a lot of people. Yet, for a time in my life, I would argue I loved endings and new beginnings so much that I became addicted to the energy and applications of the Death card. While the card is widely understood to represent a metaphorical death, most people still look upon those times with fear, regret, and sadness. In my own life however, these times have led to rebirth and reinvention and are followed by periods of intense, ecstatic joy. This is, in part, a personal addiction to new beginnings, but it's also because the Death card symbolizes what I believe deep down to be most true. We sometimes lose so we can gain. We must kill off parts of ourselves to become our best self. We must accept the cycles of death in our lives with dignity in order to usher in the following eras of rebirth.

Because I take a sunnier view of Death overall and frequently focus more on the opportunity for change and growth that comes with it, my queered version reflects that optimism. In a queer person's life, there is constant change and death, starting with the coming out process. When we accept that we are gay, for example, we are closing the door on the possibility of the societally approved heteronormative life. I actually had a really hard time with this. I attempted to go back into the closet with two different men. I was raised female, which meant I was so sure I wanted a husband, kids, and a white picket fence. I didn't though, and I wasn't meant to have those things. So yes, with Death we are ending dreams. We are also stepping into a life where we get to be who we truly are. I have known big, huge love of all kinds in my life. I have been head over heels for some of the greatest women and genderqueer people you will ever meet. I met my soulmate, a genderqueer person whose relationship to me is totally platonic but who would scour the ends of the Earth looking for me if I went missing. I have repaired bonds with given family and dived headfirst into the familial queer love of chosen family. None of that, absolutely none of it, would have happened if I hadn't seen Death's function in my life: to kill off those old dreams so that I can embrace something totally different.

Another huge example of necessary Death in queer life is the one felt when transgender people transition. In fact, this is the number one card that comes up for clients in or on the verge of transition. These clients are entering a totally new life, but that does mean saying good-bye to their old life, right down to their name (I mean, it's called a deadname for a reason). While some trans people do feel a sense of nostalgia and sadness when thinking about life pre-transition, across the board they recognized how necessary and important this manifestation of Death is. For most of my clients going through this, the Death card is a welcome sight as it brings with it the end of an era where everything was wrong.

When you are able to live your truth, your previous life ends. That time of secrets, lies, or hiding dies. We have seen this narrative play out both in art, film, and entertainment as well as in our own queer friends' lives many times. The actual Death is often sudden. It is difficult and painful to feel and accept. Once we embrace Death's hand, though, the rebirth follows. That rebirth is what so many of our queer dreams are made of. It's that rebirth that gives me such a loving view of the Death card in the first place. Death is unequivocally about Death. It is about endings, period. Yet, I still love that. Shaking toxic friends feels good. Moving out of queerphobic hellholes of towns feels amazing. Being yourself is magickal. Yet, reading that for someone else can inspire so much fear in anticipation. Do think about what happens after Death, because *that* is stunning.

Of course, some Death is painful and hard. In a reading that is not queer, should this indicate a literal Death of a loved one, of course we are sad even if we believe their afterlife situation will be wonderful. When we have to leave a career because our name has been dirtied, or leave a partner because they are an addict, we get to be sad about that. We get to grieve about it. For a queer seeker, there is a real possibility of losing loved ones as you come into your own. These too are real, tragic deaths of relationships and that hurts, and those are deaths that we mourn. For queer seekers this is extra painful, because we have often spent a very long time denying and suppressing our emotions. Death encourages us to grieve and to feel that pain. Death wants us to acknowledge when it hurts. It is only through processing our emotions in real time that we truly heal and recover, and Death is almost always wanting us to heal into better people.

Everyone loses relationships with friends and family in their lives, but it is fairly unique to queer people to lose those relationships because of who you are. For some, this unfortunately extends beyond lost relationships. It is not uncommon for someone who is not straight and cisgender to come out or be outed at work and lose one's job. It is not uncommon to be outed to your landlord and lose your home. Death comes up here too, and like the losses of relationships, these are hard deaths. We do not want to see the silver lining. We do not want to be told it's okay. And that's okay too. Death does promise rebirth and new beginnings, but it is still a card of Death. You do not need to think ahead now. Take a deep breath and figure out how you want to bury your dead. Do you bury them peacefully, releasing transphobic ex-friends to their own karma and moving on in your own life? Or do you let things die with all of the fight in you, flinging lawsuits at bad employers and setting fire to the things that have caused you pain? Death does not prescribe the right or proper way to grieve; it insists, patiently, only that you do grieve.

TEMPERANCE

The Temperance card is a beautiful, uplifting card of balance and harmony. It is also a problem card for many readers. Balance and harmony seem like straightforward ideas, but it's hard to read those ideas for other people and guess at what balance means to the seeker and what area of their life needs it. As I've matured as a person and reader, I tend to advise people to make sure they're including all aspects of their life when planning their days, weeks, next five years. It is also a card I have come to understand spiritually. This is a card of finding a center to come back to. It's a card of patience, and I

find that much more applicable to my spiritual life. If a deity or energy isn't speaking to me, Temperance comes to tell me to be patient. If I am feeling frazzled throughout a busy workday, this card is a reminder to take a step back and move more slowly.

The Temperance card is meant to be calming and affirming on sight. As such, most incarnations of the card include visions of rainbows. From Christian mythology (which the *Rider-Waite-Smith Tarot* is based on), a rainbow was a promise that God wouldn't drown the whole world again. More straightforwardly, rainbows are a promise that the rain always ends. This card, then, teaches a crucial lesson about staying balanced and harmonious within ourselves and within the world around us. We must remember that the rain always ends, and when we cannot remember that, we need to find that rainbow or promise so we do remember. It is on this note that we begin queering this card.

While balance and inner peace are important for everyone, these lessons from Temperance hit a little harder for those of any marginalized identity, and that brings us right into meeting a seeker's needs in a reading. It's important to recognize how much harder finding harmony in your life and self may be when you're trapped in a situation where you have to be closeted, where you are unsafe, or if you are at a point where you're not even sure who you are or how you identify. Additionally, outside clatter from queerphobic people in our lives and harmful media messages can create a wholly unbalanced self, no matter how hard we work to stay centered. Frequently, if Temperance shows up in readings around those topics, it's likely doing so as a reminder that finding a balance is both necessary and difficult now. There are times, then, that Temperance goes from being a peaceful image of someone filling one cup without depleting another, to being a message of someone juggling those cups and hoping all the water doesn't run out. How we handle that as readers is obviously totally different. The card is a little bit of a wake-up call. Maybe we are trying too hard or juggling when we could be letting things stand still. And in a very straightforward way, we see this card reminding a queer person that self-care is even more important for the marginalized. That seeker should incorporate a meditative practice or a mantra that affirms themselves and their identities, and brings them to a peaceful center.

The Temperance idea of balance shifts slightly when we start looking at our careers. In this case, the card's lesson is that you should be seeking a situation where you can combine the things you love with the things you're good at. That's a balance that should be easy to find, but we don't exactly live in a world where following your dreams is encouraged. Some of us have no idea until later in life that the careers we want are totally doable—you just have to use the skill set you have to make it so. For queer people, it's scary enough to come out and start a life where we can be happy in our body, or romantic life, or both. It is sometimes even harder to admit we want to walk a much different career path than our parents would choose for us. With Temperance though, you can absolutely use your love of painting to make a living if you're willing to teach or take commercial jobs. You can absolutely pursue being queer Oprah if you're willing to use your medical background to work your way up through some medically oriented talk shows. You can absolutely take your skills as an artist to the protest and help others create a picture of a better, more liberated world . . . or just help the other protesters decorate their posters.

There are many different ways to be a queer activist or advocate. Some of us are meant to work within the system to change it. Some of us are meant to write books, make art, or otherwise find a way to increase representation. Some of us are meant to fight on the front lines. Some of us are simply meant to create harmony wherever we go within our queer community. Temperance frequently shows up for that last type of queer seeker as a sign that it's time to move into an activist role within your local community. You are being called on to make the world better by using your own voice and story to motivate and comfort others. This is actually the most common interpretation of this card that I've seen come up with LGBTQQIP2SA+ clients. This interpretation shows that the time to be a simple member of this community has passed. It is now time to ascend into someone who brings peace to the community, whatever that looks like for the seeker.

The Temperance card does speak to moderation as well as balance, peace, and harmony. As we seek to retain balance in our lives as queer people, that means we can't fill one cup by depleting another. You cannot solely pour your energy into activist work or into matters concerning your gender or sexual identity. It is so tempting to do so, I know. I frequently have to pull back from things because I've lost my sense of who I am beyond queer. Even as I, and many of us, make our money, our art, and our lives around queer things, it is important to nurture all sides of that beyond the identity itself. I'm still a sibling, a member of my neighborhood community, and a huge comic books fan. All of that is an integral part of who I am, and if I am getting Temperance a lot, it's usually time to step away from my closet of rainbow flags and jump into the community garden with the kids who live next door.

The most important part of the Temperance card for LGBTQQIP2SA+ people is the concept of moderation. Any queer community has a really rad and probably large sober community within it. Which is to say that many queer seekers are living in sobriety and have a history of alcohol or drug abuse. The literal lesson of moderation within the Temperance card is to monitor your vices and escape mechanisms closely. Drug and alcohol abuse is a fact with any group in society, but I know for queer clients this issue has specifically come up as a reminder not to go too far, or for those in sobriety as a reminder that life balance is ultra-key to continued sobriety. Temperance could also be a clue for you as a reader that the person you're reading for is in sobriety, so be careful how you speak of indulgence or before recommending seeking community in an alcohol-soaked hangout. This is an affirming card for those living in sobriety. There are many other cards that indicate falling off the wagon, so assure them that while they are struggling, there are rainbows in their life they can look to for hope. They can get through this rough patch. Encourage them to use any meditative or mindfulness practice they've picked up, but also assure them (or yourself, if you're just reading for you) that they have done great work and will continue to thrive in sobriety.

Temperance is another Major Arcana card that comes up frequently in regards to sexual and gender fluidity. It's a card of balancing multiple cups, and the lesson or vision of fluidity literally runs through the card. I see Temperance pop up most often in situations where, for example, the person you've been seeing is not a gender you thought you were into, or you started randomly finding new genders attractive. It also tends to show up for genderfluid seekers (like myself), though not as often as a couple of the other cards in the tarot. The lesson here is no doubt to accept this moment, time, or era of fluidity. Maybe it's a permanent part of who you are, but for now just enjoy this feeling, and trust that it will lead you where it needs to.

Temperance is one of the trickier cards to read for someone else. One person's balance is another's chaos. This is arguably one of the most individualized cards in the deck. That makes it a great fit for the rich culture of individuality we see in a good queer community, but does make reading it a bit of a puzzle. You can certainly delve a little deeper and rely on other cards to fill in the bigger picture in those moments. It's important to remember, though, that tarot, like any metaphysical art, isn't always a clear or tangible thing with a clear-cut result. Sometimes you're being called to just sit and simmer on the word *harmony* and see what springs forth. There is a temptation of modern seers to make our craft legit by assigning it foolproof secular value. Sometimes that just isn't there, and frequently the Temperance card has a deeper, more spiritual message for us that we are commanded to mull over until the clouds part and it becomes clear.

THE DEVIL

In tarot, The Devil is a card that, on first glance, clients normally assume means that someone or something is *bad* or *wrong*. The card indicates that a situation is tempting but not good for you, or that an oppressive force is determined to keep you down. This obviously comes from Christian mythos wherein the Devil is evil and Jesus is good. If you look closer at the Bible though, the Devil shows up more as something meant to tempt God-loving folk away from their chosen path and into something else entirely. The *what* is never clear. Even in non-queered readings, I usually choose to talk about this card as temptation or an alternative viewpoint—one that isn't necessarily bad, but that does need to be weighed carefully against the path laid out in front of you. Other keywords for The Devil frequently include bondage or addiction, so this card can also be an opportunity to break negative cycles.

When queering this card, our first exploration is going to be on what oppressive forces are at play in a querent's life. It's easy to jump to homophobic parents, transphobic employers, and biphobic partners, and, of course, there is a chance that The Devil is indicating these things. The Major Arcana cards frequently want us to delve into and repair our relationship with ourselves. Digging deeper that way, there's a good chance with The Devil that we're looking at internalized queerphobia. We could also be seeing that self-imposed expectations of what *being* queer means are pulling the client out of whack. I have an email client who lives in a very rural area in a state that's not very progressive. For her, new relationships frequently show The Devil card, and she finally confided one day that she wasn't comfortable moving forward in relationships because it wasn't safe to walk down the street holding hands with her partner. In this case, her town's culture was the oppressive Devil that was keeping her down—but so was the way she internalized it.

Over time, my relationship with The Devil has become more nuanced. I mentioned earlier that this card shows up, not as something particularly bad, just something tempting but not for me. The Biblical Devil (although it's worth noting this figure is never actually called that in the Bible) wants to make us question our faith, strength, and the road we're headed down. Certainly this interpretation of The Devil is applicable to queer people. I have seen non-monosexual and even transgender clients feel tempted to go back in the closet when their dream job or partner shows up, or when a neglectful parent reappears and the client wants to appease them. I have seen people who know they are polyamorous decide to hold off on opening up a relationship because of a number of difficult situations. Now, these choices are not always bad, and if they show up in a reading full of happy cards, we talk about moving at your own pace and making your own choices. When those choices show up in a reading where The Devil shows up, however, it is definitely time to examine if this situation or relationship is pulling you away from being your true self in an unhealthy or constricting way.

As we've queered the tarot, we've seen cards normally held in a positive or affectionate regard become darker or more negative. This was true of The Hierophant and Justice, for example. Queering cards means questioning the positive and negative connotations associated with cards, and that also means some negative cards do become positive. Temptation and indulgence are not always bad. If a client who once struggled to be healthy has been depriving themselves of all sweets or salty treats and gets The Devil alongside cards of balance, my job may be to remind them that balance is key to life. I'd advise they should be easier on themselves about their diet and give in to indulgences once in a while. A common way I've seen this idea manifest in readings for queer clients (and for myself) is in the idea of embracing our spot in the queer community with lots of celebrations at gay bars or house parties full of LGBTQQIP2SA+ people. As long as one is able to do this responsibly, there is nothing wrong with overindulging occasionally while going out. Similarly, if someone has been in the closet or hasn't fully realized their identity until recently, The Devil can show up as a note that it's completely fine and even well aspected to indulge sexually. This can include experimentation, if that time of full realization isn't complete, but can also simply indicate a time where sexual activity is frequent and varied. If the surrounding cards are positive, please feel free to indulge in all the no-strings fun you desire. I personally feel that this is an important part of a human growth process, but we live in a society where owning our sexuality—whatever that sexuality is—is considered wrong. The Devil and I have frequently worked together in a reading to break down some of that sexual repression for clients.

Finally, if anyone reading knows the tarot very well, they might realize there's a word frequently associated with The Devil that I've been avoiding—bondage. That's because I want the idea of The Devil indicating a positive relationship with bondage to have its own space. Of all the aforementioned examples and interpretations of The Devil in a queer reading, the number one way it shows itself as a positive force is when I am working with a client who strongly identifies with either a dominant or submissive role in relationships, and for whom BDSM is a substantial part of their life. In this case, many of the ideas we've talked about—oppression, temptation, allowing for sexuality—feed into the idea of The Devil freeing us or highlighting positive associations with bondage. The Devil can be about a consensually controlling force as opposed to the oppressive energy many see in it. The first few times I saw The Devil surrounded by happy Cups (indicating love) and Wands (indicating passion), I was a little confused. Many years later, it's abundantly clear that when this happens, we are reading for someone who either loves to control or be controlled, particularly in a bondage setting, and we cannot look at that as a solely unhealthy thing when we're pushing for sexual liberation.

Sex positivity and indulgence are not something most societies are comfortable with. Queering The Devil is one of the most important steps to queering the tarot for so many reasons. The milestones and steps in a queer person's life are so different from those for our cisgender and straight friends. That gives us slightly different interpretations of The Devil. It's crucial that we take a sex-positive look at this card, separate from many of the Judeo-Christian ideals that made it into traditional tarot decks and interpretations. Once you're looking at the card through that sex-positive lens, even readings not about sex or relationships take a different spin where that becomes the metaphor. Then we're looking at a story of indulging after a time of having to hold back, or a story of enjoying a position in an area of your life where someone else is leading.

So much of queering the tarot comes down to breaking down our own misconceptions and biases on what relationships should and shouldn't be, or do and do not look like. The Devil is no exception. Not every reading will automatically queer

The Devil to make it more positive, though. There are very real oppressors that hold LGBTQQIP2SA+ querents in the negatively aspected view of bondage. There is often harmful temptation meant to pull us off our path. I would be remiss to not bring up the substantial sober community within the larger queer community, and truthfully I have a number of sober clients for whom The Devil shows up in its more traditional form. Many modern readers, myself included, believe that tarot readings should have a more conversational aspect. That conversation is the second key to cracking how to queer this card in your particular reading. The first key is putting on those sex-positive glasses and experimenting with viewing the card from that lens.

THE TOWER

More than any other, The Tower is a card that freaks people out when it shows up in a reading, and there's good reason for that. Traditionally this card indicates destruction and chaos. The Tower brings down an entire life, albeit one we've built on a false foundation. The Tower can and will shake up your whole world. It can bring huge epiphanies that can alter your entire life path. I've seen it indicate literal concerns with one's home as well, which is never what one wants to hear when they sit down for a reading. As I tell every client regardless of identity, it's important to remember that The Tower brings down only the things in our lives that are built on a shaky foundation. It can be really hard to process and deal with the destruction it bears, but it's also an opportunity to rebuild something stronger and better. The Tower can also indicate a major shake-up as opposed to abject destruction; for those whose lives have become mundane or for people who've become complacent about less-than-great circumstances, this card can actually be a relief if you're willing to reshape your whole world.

Queering The Tower starts with looking at what those specific shake-ups or false foundations might be for an LGBTQQIP2SA+ person. If one has chosen or is forced to remain closeted or even just quiet about their queer identity, it's possible this card is predicting that an unfortunate outing or confrontation might occur. Like with our straight and cisgender seekers, we can see a major relationship falling apart, so knowing the culture of queer relationships is important when addressing this reality of The Tower. When queering the tarot, the querent or their partner might find that they are the one about to tear down The Tower by coming out. I've seen this most often with gender transitions and poly identities. The relationships in their lives could change dramatically, and in many cases could even be ending. Sometimes the truth hurts. As a reader I strive for empowerment, but The Tower is usually not kind. Few things in life are totally bad or totally good though, and the fall of a tower built on something false is, and should be, liberating for most queer seekers. You get to rebuild your life as yourself, on your own terms. Yes, we see heartache and pain and misery. Grieve. Mourn. Cry. Know when it's time to rebuild, and know that rebuilding as your queerest, most authentic self is absolutely your best bet.

Alternatively, my favorite experience of queering the tarot means looking at the card totally differently. If queering the tarot means taking not only LGBTQQIP2SA+, kink, and polyam identities into consideration but also the idea that the queer community is one built on a different value system from the straight patriarchy we live under, it's very possible that The Tower becomes a positive force for change in a once-maligned person or organization's heart or policies. It's possible you are being named as a huge force for much-needed change in the world. It's possible that if something catastrophic happens you come out on top. It's possible too that you knock down your own Tower built on half-truths and misplaced trust, and move on to rebuild your life into something so much more beautiful than you ever could have imagined. You now get a life that is genuine and full of queer family and allies, and you get the support structure you deserve. It's even possible with The Tower that you're being called on to create that support system. When those Towers fall for those who don't have a safety net, you can provide that. That is powerful. The Tower is powerful and you are powerful, and together you can be one hell of a force for good. I've discussed before how cards indicating tradition and institutions can be very negative for queer people. The flip side of that is cards like this—cards that many would fear when they come up in a reading. Instead, The Tower could be calling you to greatness, begging you to burn down the institutions that would keep us marginalized, and building something new and beautiful in their place.

THE STAR

When I started the *Queering the Tarot* article series, I primarily wanted to examine the cards individually and see how they would apply specifically to LGBTQQIP2SA+ querents, as well as share stories from my life and those of my clients to see how the applications manifest. While this is still a key component of my writing, the connections between the cards have become just as powerful as the cards themselves. The Star is our next card, and we can't truly examine it without recalling the sometimes traumatic events of The Tower. The Star is frequently thought of as what comes after a period

when everything is falling down around us. While the picture is always peaceful, in my mind I have always thought an ideal Star card would be the same picture surrounded by the rubble of The Tower. It would have just as much hope as traditional interpretations of The Star, but without denying what got us here.

Traditionally The Star indicates hope. It shows a slight illumination in a dark time, like a star guiding you home. The Star card usually shows an image of a woman nourishing the Earth and being nourished in return, a potential statement on the infinite resources available to us, and their cyclical nature. Renewal and refreshment are also indicated with this card, and The Star promises us a fresh burst of energy. Vacations are often indicated with this card, along with anything that makes us feel as if we've hit a reset button. This is one of the cards in the deck that is harder to separate from its spiritual root, as the card itself can mean simply *spirituality* or comfort via spiritual matters. You're truly blessed by the Divine (whatever or whoever that is to you) in this time.

In a queer reading, this card almost always comes up after we've gone through a rough time. It might not always be as devastating as The Tower, but it is hard to ignore the feeling of loss and being left to stand on your own that The Tower leaves behind and how that uniquely affects LGBTQQIP2SA+ querents when queering The Star. Without The Tower of being outed or coming out in unsupportive environments, you don't have that moment of hope and clarity where you realize that either you can make life work on your own, or that you do have support around you to rebuild from. Recognizing the milestones that queer seekers face and how The Star as a source of hope, illumination, or renewal would show up for them is an easy enough line to draw—it is essentially, after all, the breakthrough that comes when all has fallen. Politically, it's been a rough couple of years. We have more or less been living in a period of Tower after Tower, especially when we are marginalized. The Star doesn't deny any of that reality, but does lead us to look at the signs of hope and change all around us, even if this card itself is one of the only signs we get that things will turn around.

The Star is a card that deals pretty heavily with the infinite resources of the universe and what's available to us. In very straightforward readings for LGBTQQIP2SA+ querents, The Star also shows up to guide us toward community resources. It doesn't just show up as a promise that those resources are there—it's an actual advice card encouraging you to seek out the services or social groups that you need. This can include anything from a gay bar to a trans-friendly therapist, but if The Star is present, your search for that resource should be fruitful.

The matter of spirituality is a difficult one for many queer people. Many of us in the West grew up in oppressive Christian households or are acutely aware that the rights and dignities we do not have in large part stay absent from our lives because of the stronghold of the Christian Right in our society. For that reason, many have abandoned or turned their back not only on Christianity, but also on spirituality as a whole. Some may never miss it, and atheism is a perfectly valid belief if that works for you. For many though, spirituality is a source of inspiration and connection to spirit, and a crucial part of who we are and how we view the world. When that's taken from you or you lose that faith, your life can feel out of balance. All too often, losing your faith feels like losing yourself as well. So, for many in this community, The Star shows up to indicate that it is safe and it's time for the querent to seek out a spiritual path. Seeking out that spiritual path will look a lot different this time around. This is a new sense of spirit and a new road we're walking down. None of the traps that were hurting us in our old faith are meant to be here now. This is a time to try on many different hats, spiritually speaking, and see what works for you.

Spirituality often moves in cycles in our lives and in the world at large. Right now we are seeing a huge uptick in queer and trans people turning to Pagan paths and even being willing to experiment with paths other may view as darker. This path, for me and many others, has led to a sense of faith in self and spirit that was so lost for so long. The Star promises refreshment and renewal, and we find that when we start looking beyond a faith that has hurt us for connection and spirituality.

Finally, The Star as a card about faith directly addresses one of the biggest epidemics sweeping any community of marginalized people—low self-esteem or lack of faith in ourselves. Many times when The Tower falls, good or bad, it was for reasons beyond our control. The Star comes to let us know that anything we made out of the rubble, we made on our own, and to remind us how much more we can build. We have an idea and a focus for our life now, thanks to that illumination from The Star, and it is time to create the path we want out of it. Hold tight to your faith in yourself when this card shows up. We live in a pretty nasty society where gender and sexual minorities are concerned. Even when legal rights are obtained, our dignities are affronted every day, but we are so strong and so beautiful in the face of that. The Star shows up to remind us of this, to remind us to keep fighting the good fight—whether it's for the community or just for ourselves. More importantly, The Star shows up to remind us how capable we really are, and how many miracles we can create by learning to believe in ourselves again.

THE MOON

For me, as a stereotypical Pisces, The Moon has always been one of the most important tarot cards in the whole deck. In so many ways this card sums up the tarot's intention and purpose in and of itself. This card indicates our own psychic power and brings connection to the moon and to water. This is a card of deep intuitive knowledge that encourages us to dig deep into our subconscious to find the answers we're looking for. Because of this card's connection to intuition, it often surfaces when someone in our lives is being deceptive. I reject this interpretation sometimes, because The Moon is traditionally the feminine face of the Divine, and The Sun is its masculine counterpart. I refuse to demonize the feminine face of the Divine, and that does mean rejecting this function of the card. It does have its place though. When we are talking about rooting around in our subconscious and our intuition, what we often uncover are all of those ways we deceive ourselves. This is where low self-esteem lives. This is where that part of us that stops us from taking bold risks or listening to our soul when it's crying out for purpose thrives. Learning about this defensive part of ourselves is an important part of a growth and healing cycle, and The Moon just wants to prod us further down a path to healing.

The Moon does illuminate things when you are looking for answers, but unlike the bright, warm glow of the sun, the moon guides us with slivers of light and odd persistence, requiring us to go deeper into ourselves for the answers we seek. The Moon represents our shadow self, the side that shows when we are home alone with ourselves and we don't have to put on a show or a happy face for anyone. Again, I absolutely adore this card. I love that it represents a mixed up Piscean duality by indicating both illusions at play and an energy calling you to face that illusion head-on. That seeming contrast leads to something else entirely—a concise message to listen to your subconscious and your intuition, and an encouragement to go deeper into your own depths. The High Priestess alluded to knowledge that was within us the whole time, and The Moon sees it slowly come to light.

It is without a doubt time to listen to your intuition when The Moon comes up in a reading. It is 100 percent a sign that you know the answers you're seeking. What's blocking you from seeing that? Why don't you trust that inner voice? What are your literal dreams telling you while you're fast asleep that you refuse to see in your waking life? These are the questions The Moon begs us to ask ourselves, and the reason she doesn't give us answers to them is because we already know the answers.

As we look at queering The Moon, we go back to The Star's call for us to explore alternative spiritualities. The Moon can be calling us specifically to a spirituality where a divine feminine is honored, instead of the more popular (in present-day society) divine masculine. Of course worshiping or praying to a divine feminine isn't a queer-specific calling and not all LGBTQQIP2SA+ people will be called to such a religion. However, it is a common experience when your sexual or gender identity isolates you from a more patriarchal religion that a more fluid, feminine one would call to you. While this card's spiritual elements indicating intuition and prophetic dreams don't seem like they would be altered that dramatically because someone is LGBTQQIP2SA+, many in our community who come from oppressive backgrounds where we are told listening to ourselves is wrong, that who we think we are isn't okay, that our very perception of ourselves is up for discussion by people who aren't us, have a tough time listening to themselves. The Moon may show up over and over again for people who have been trained not to trust themselves. If you're getting this card a lot and it's getting frustrating, don't despair. You are not intentionally blocking out your subconscious or intuition. You just have to dig deeper into that shadow self to get there and allow The Moon to guide you along the way.

Regardless of one's gender or sexual identity, The Moon brings big things to the surface, things we often let bubble up only when we're alone. An important alternative interpretation to note, then, is as an indicator of past trauma such as abuse or sexual assault. I bring this up not only because I don't think it gets talked about enough in relation to this card, but also because queer people all too frequently accept trauma as part of our lives and suppress the very real effects it may have on us. Even worse, LGBTQQIP2SA+ people often do not feel supported, included, or even welcome in the few spaces or within the resources that exist for trauma recovery. I have seen this card bring tears to people's eyes even when they have no idea what it means. As we dig through the reading, trauma often comes to light. Again, The Moon's primary job is not just to bring painful things to the surface—it wants us to heal. That's why everything we try to suppress keeps bubbling up. Listen to your Divine, do some dreamwork, and spend some time sitting with your intuition to begin healing from these unfortunate circumstances.

The Moon does bring us wonderful things once we start on our path to healing. The Moon's illumination and the concept of healing in the tarot are closely linked. When this card shows up, the moonlight will guide us to those healing forces if we listen to ourselves and those we trust. Unlike The Tower or even the positive-but-huge Wheel of Fortune, The Moon allows you to take things slowly. It's here encouraging you to process and pushing you to get in tune spiritually so that you can guide yourself through the next stages of healing. The Moon loves LGBTQQIP2SA+ seekers, and wants us to feel confident in our voice as we move down our path.

THE SUN

Following The Moon, naturally, is The Sun. The Sun (in contrast with The Moon) leaves little to the imagination. It shines brightly, illuminating all in its path. In our secular lives, it's generally a positive omen in most areas, but even more so for creative people, those looking to start a family, individuals who've had it rough and need an energy shift, and for people with questions related to health. This is a truly radiant card, guaranteeing that whatever your question, it is aspected well. I actually kind of hate when this card comes up in readings for other people because it's so positive that I feel like

I'm blowing smoke. If I pull it in regards to my own career, health, or love life though, I'm pretty ecstatic. As advice this card is still pretty great. Go have fun, or maybe yes, take that big risk. It also advises us to stay positive since we are on exactly the right trajectory.

As we begin queering The Sun though, we do see some shadow work or darker themes. I mentioned that The Sun leaves little to the imagination. While that's often a good thing, if you've been avoiding facing a core aspect of your identity or if you've been wanting or needing to stay in a closet, you could be outed or forced to come to terms with this now. No card is flawlessly positive all the time, and if you're asking about an element of your life or identity that you're not ready to bring your gender or sexual identity into, having The Sun shine brightly on the issue can be a bad thing. That being said, the card is *usually* sunny and positive, so I can guarantee you'll be in a much better situation in six months because of these events than you ever could have dreamed.

Generally The Sun is a very positive time for manifesting and pulling what you want into your life. I often liken it to a King Midas card, but that story had a dark side, too. You can have too much of a good thing, and it's important to be careful what you wish for. LGBTQQIP2SA+ seekers are not any more likely to be attracted to dangerous partners than anyone else. We aren't more likely to use our determination to will them into our arms than the general population but . . . we are *as* likely to do those things. For our community too, there is a lack of resources for dealing with the fallout of such relationships to take into account. This can be applied across the board to all areas of our lives. And, because queer people sometimes separate ourselves from our inner voice or intuition, we can manifest and wish things into being that aren't all that great for us. I reiterate if this card comes up surrounded by darker cards, be careful what you wish for right now, because you're going to get it.

On the neutral side of The Sun, this card deals quite a bit with the divine masculine. It often shows up in readings about one's spiritual path for queer seekers who are still steeped in or are finding their way back to a Judeo-Christian version of God or spirituality. When we are trying to reconcile our faith with any backlash we may have received or internalized guilt we may be carrying because of our gender or sexual identities, The Sun promises that the same faith can help us heal moving forward. This is positively aspected then, but some querents may still have negative associations with such a God or carry guilt from growing up in a culture with a traditional mind-set. This is still a spiritual path that will ultimately work out well, though. There may be some emotional pitfalls to deal with along the way, but we are being pushed back to that sense of spirituality.

In questions directly regarding gender or sexual identity, this card does hint at masculinity. If The Sun alone shows up when someone is directly inquiring about their identity, I wouldn't feel comfortable making that call. However, if other cards with masculine energy show up, I know to advise toward a masculine-of-center partner, identity, or presentation. This card does come up quite often for transgender men, gay men, butch women, non-binary people, and bisexual and pansexual people as a way to guide them toward their best option or affirm their intuition that the masculine is right, right now.

The Sun is most often a happy card, and I mentioned earlier that it is generally a good omen for families, and certainly indicates children for those seeking parenthood. This is especially true for the same-sex couples, couples where one or both partners are transgender, and polyamorous families I read for. Often when people in these relationships are thinking about children, they experience darkness and tough decisions, rough starts, and mishaps on the journey to bringing children into their lives. They might feel frustrated with the entire process, and questioning if they should give up. The Sun does promise that those darker days are behind us (or will be soon), and that the family we dream of is coming. Furthermore The Sun assures us that the family unit will thrive and grow long after the children in question are safely in your home.

In general when looking at queering the tarot, it's most important to remember that LGBTQQIP2SA+ querents don't always walk the same life path or hit the same milestones as those who are straight and cisgender, so the biggest queering of The Sun is just taking that altered path into account when it comes up. A positive omen for a queer seeker could be much harder won than for someone else, and is frequently following a time when they were forced into closets or trapped in places where they couldn't shine as brightly because they couldn't be themselves safely. It is not well-advised, when sitting with a client who's been through the queer wringer and asking about coping mechanisms or what they have to look forward to, to start chanting "positivity" like one is likely to do otherwise. It's much harder to embrace positivity when you've spent much of your life fighting to be yourself and are still fighting for full human rights in your society. I see a lot of trauma survivors, and I wouldn't tell them, "Don't worry, things are going to be fine!" I also wouldn't say that to someone living through the daily trauma of being marginalized even when a super-happy card shows up.

Circling back to The Sun's promise of family, warmth, and community, we again touch on the super-queer concept of chosen family, and how often that is community wide. If we are lonely, scared, frustrated, or moving to a new city, The Sun shows up to promise that there is a thriving queer community there for us. It isn't going to take us long to find it, and when we do, it will shift the other energy in our lives. This means new romantic prospects, lots of fun and adventure, and likely some good career opportunities and chances to get healthy. The Sun is such a wonderful, promising card and if there's anything queer seekers need right now it's the joy promised within this one. If you're pulling the card, take a deep breath, release the tension in your shoulders, and take that huge leap forward you've been hoping for.

JUDGMENT

Judgment is a tricky card because *judgment* is a word that has many negative connotations regardless of whether or not someone is queer. The metaphor in a more traditional deck is troubling to many—the archangel Gabriel sounds his trumpet, and the time of the final judgment is upon us. This word itself, as well as its religious aspect, can be especially troublesome to those who are queer, having spent most of their lives trying to avoid or heal from judgment, and in many cases needing to heal the scars inflicted by organized Christianity itself. This card is meant to be positive, though. Judgment brings big moments and realizations, but those moments provide us with absolution and make our soul's purpose crystal clear.

Normally if Judgment is in your reading, you are at the end of a phase of life. That means it's time to do some self-examination, process the lessons you've learned, and move forward in your life as an improved (if not new) person. This card is a strong indicator that you need to heed a spiritual calling or that it's time to start living up to your ideals. Judgment further indicates a time where your karmic debt is resetting, for better or worse. That's where the judgment comes in. The really great, wonderful energy you've put in will come back now, but so will the negative. This can be a card of rebirth because of this reset, and in some of my contemporary decks there's celebration at having closed one chapter of your life and being joyous at the opportunity to ascend to a better version of yourself.

To queer this deck we have to look at it one of two ways—either both the reader and querent can get past the negative connotations the word judgment has to queer communities, or they can't. It's not helpful to try to push someone who's really not responding well to a card, and in queering the tarot or taking any sort of identity-based approach, it's much more helpful to take your cues from the seeker. This is especially true when you're your own seeker. Please do not ever push yourself to get over something in a self-guided reading. Go with your own gut. In this case we look at what Judgment as a card means and what the seeker is seeing in it, then find the common ground. For example, someone recently aware of their own queerness might have received a higher calling to live their truth, but they may also have been addled with the realization that their faith community wouldn't be supportive. Alternatively, someone who's out and proud may get a spiritual calling to get back into a more traditional faith, and may have even found an open faith community. Unfortunately LGBTQQIP2SA+ friends are not always understanding or compassionate about one's need for religion, especially within a sect they find limiting. In both of these cases, the card's calling to living a higher ideal and the querent's understanding of judgment and the harm it does are true, and both show up in the reading.

Another queering of Judgment comes in looking at that karmic reset. All of us have negative energy that smacks us in the face when we least expect it. I'm not proud of everything I did when I was in the closet. Hell, I'm still not proud of everything I do when I react from a place of fear. I'm not my highest self in these moments, and when a negatively aspected Judgment shows up looking to make me atone for that, I have to either make my peace with it or try to correct course. This means healing is needed for queer seekers. This is about going back through the previous few cards and walking that healing path again until we arrive back at Judgment, prouder and more sure of starting a new chapter in our lives.

Then there's that idea of ascension or moving forward. That obviously looks different when we see this card in a more negative light. As a reader you might be used to the Death card showing up to say, "Hey, this thing has to be over. Time to move on anyway, even if it's hard," but for queer people it also absolutely can and does show up as the Judgment card. Judgment shows up to say, "You're right. Your family, friends, current partner, workplace, or others, *are* judging you. You have to ascend and move forward anyway." It's a harder truth than we sometimes see in this card, but it's an important understanding of it.

Of course for anyone, regardless of identity, Judgment brings lessons of evaluation and reflection, and that does show up for queer people just as it does for others. We're back now at positive associations of Judgment, but still very queer. When we look at a period of reflection through a queer lens, those lessons look different. Living up to our ideals can have much more to do with speaking our truth, being willing to call out queerphobic language or jokes, or trying harder to give back to groups or communities that helped us get and stay on our feet when we were struggling. These are all huge callings. Judgment doesn't mess around. If you're getting this card as a queer person, even positively aspected, it's time to step up. The amazing, fantastic flip side of being called to step up though is that you are ready to step up. It takes a lot to get to this place, but you did it. That's awesome. Celebrate like this card calls you to do, then get to work.

Tarot is often a tool for *big messages* from the Divine, but sometimes even the heaviest cards show up much more innocently. In the very tangible, very mundane, Judgment can be indicating we're ready for the next step in our lives, even if that step is small. If you're queer in your sexual identity but haven't dated anyone yet, this card says you're ready to do so. In that vein, you could be ready for your first polyamorous relationship, or to bring someone new into your existing polyam situation. If your kink is part of your identity, there could be a very literal new skill or sexual act you're finally ready to try. For trans people, this card frequently shows up as being ready for next stage of transition (whatever that looks like to the seeker). I've worked with several transgender performing artists who haven't performed as their true selves yet, and this card has shown up to say they are ready to shirk that fear of judgment and step into the limelight. The literal visual of a trumpet, and what in many decks could be perceived as an audience, lends itself to this latter view of the card quite nicely.

Judgment is also a positive thing for queer querents when it shows up as a spiritual awakening or epiphany. This interpretation can be straightforward, and not in need of queering per se, but it can also be intensely queer and calling us to leadership in an advocacy or social group geared toward our identity (or some facet of it). It can also mean you're being called to spiritual leadership as your true, queer, beautiful self. This is terrifying to most LGBTQQIP2SA+ people. I know I wouldn't feel great leading a proper coven for fear of others' perception, so I know for those in less radical faiths it's even scarier. Spiritual matters often mean addressing our relationship with ourselves though, and we see that too with Judgment. Even with a more positive light on it, the Judgment card can still be saying that it's time to live your truth and leave behind those who don't want you to do that. There is still a melancholiness in this, but there's also a lot of light and a huge promise of a better life for doing so.

For most queer clients who can see the positive in this card, it shows up as a promise. It comes and says, "You've been judged, you've been let down, and it's been hard, but your time is coming." Karmic debt for people who have been hurt but continually rose above looks very different. It looks a lot like ascension, and it looks a lot like The Sun that was promised in that previous card. Even if we take that earlier, more negative view of Judgment, we are empowering all those who have been marginalized to step into the limelight. It is your time to shine. It is your time to turn the page. It is your time.

THE WORLD

We have arrived at the end of the Fool's Journey through the Major Arcana with The World, a card of completion and wholeness. This project, phase of your life, or even relationship is done, and that's a good thing. There is a feeling of peace and serenity as you move forward into the next phase of your life. If Judgment had you summing up the things you've learned along the way, The World sees you satisfied, stronger, and wiser as you forge your next path. Alternate interpretations of The World focus on the more literal concept of the world—namely that travel is well aspected. If The World shows up it's definitely time to see what else is out there and explore what you haven't experienced yet.

One of the first things I noticed when I began queering the tarot was how frequently The World showed up in LGBTQQIP2SA+ readings regardless of what the specific identity beyond queer was. The first logical step into queering the card was to encourage seekers to get outside of their upbringing and immediate neighborhood, community, family, and the like, when they started questioning their sexual or gender identity, and to get out into the big wide world and find communities with a lot more queerness and overall diversity running through them. This interpretation holds up today, but as our community and our understanding of sexuality and gender evolve and grow, so does our understanding of The World—both the card and the world itself. While it is significantly easier to find communities accepting of gay and lesbian people than it was even five or ten years ago, for transgender, bisexual, pansexual, genderqueer, non-binary, asexual, and so many other people, finding those communities is still really difficult. Even for gay and lesbian people, finding other gay and lesbian people or those accepting of queer people may not be enough (and it is true that there are still pockets of society that group all of us queers into one, and individuals for whom finding acceptance is still damn near impossible). It may also be time to find people who share your sexual or gender identity who also identify with you in other ways—perhaps other gay men who share your spiritual beliefs, other transgender people who love art as much as you do, or other gender non-conforming corporate employees. In all of these cases, The World is about finding or creating your own world for the first time. That's something many of us still struggle with because it does demand we get out of our comfort zone, even as that zone has started making us markedly uncomfortable.

The World also shows up for people who came into their identities a while ago but have struggled in some way to truly accept and live as themselves, or for whom a significant learning curve or transition was in place when they came out and began living their true life. The card shows up to affirm and assure such seekers that they are ready for the next phase. If this card comes up, you are ready to date as a queer person. You are about to move forward in your life after a gender transition, able to make space for all of the things that make you whole and you. You are ready to bring a new partner into a newly polyamorous situation. The cycle of discovery is done. The cycle of change and learning what that identity means is done. The cycle of accepting and loving yourself as-is is nearing completion. Queer seekers know that they feel better when they are in The World's phase. There's a significant change that has taken place, but seekers often have trouble figuring out what that means for their life. What it means is that your period of struggle or constant change is over. You are ready to step forward fresh and new—but in no way naively or youthfully like The Fool. If our Judgment card is about ascension to the next level at its base, this is the card that shows who we are and how our life manifests after that ascension. That's true regardless of one's identity, but the "who we are" and "how our life manifests" obviously look drastically different for queer people.

The World indicates achievement and success from time to time, and for those who take on activist roles or whose vocation directly correlates to their queer identity, this is even better news. Not only is that new leadership position, grant, or ad campaign aspected well, but also that you likely began doing that work for a reason—to impact the world. The World showing up in these situations is a sure sign that you are creating the change you work so diligently to create. I breathe so easily when I'm in the presence of someone who is making real, substantive change in the world. I relish the company of those who battled our whole society and made things better for all of us. I especially love reading for such people and watching The World show up as promise of that manifestation.

This is a card where wisdom and optimism reenter your life and allow you to walk peacefully and as one with the world around you. For a queer seeker, this likely means your identity and sense of self are stronger than they've ever been—a triumph in and of itself for most of us. The World likely also indicates that your community ties are strong, and if they aren't, that getting out and seeking your community is brilliantly aspected. The World means the struggles and pain of this last chapter of your life have come to a close and you have come out on top. You are ready to move forward in your fabulous queer life and take your place in The World. You didn't get to close this chapter easily, but you will be able to do so peacefully. Even better news is that you get to enjoy the next phase of that fabulously queer life exponentially more.

QUEERING
THE
MINOR ARCANA

2

THE SUIT OF WANDS

In the tarot, cards are generally separated into two parts—the Major Arcana and the Minor Arcana. The Major Arcana are considered more about archetypes—those things the Divine brings about, or the bigger picture themes and ideas for you to focus on as you navigate your journey. The Minor Arcana, then, are cards that focus on smaller picture things. Either they look at specific areas of life or help problem-solve more minor (in the grand scheme of things) issues. They focus on the Earthly or mundane, whereas the Majors are often more spiritually or philosophically inclined. Because these are often *lower bearing* cards, and because often one card's meaning or relevance is correlated to the cards that precede or follow it, we won't cover each of the cards individually.

I wanted to start with the Wands, because, in my experience, they change in some of the most expansive and subversive ways. Wands are cards of Fire. Fire can burn away harmful things. It can also start blowing out of control and cause as much damage as it meant to help. It can also go out entirely if we aren't careful. Fire needs to be nurtured, noticed, and loved. It also needs to be taken seriously as a threat, a weapon, or anything else it presents as. Fire in its most raw form is passion, determination, intuition, and energy. It is action oriented, requiring quick decisions and fast work. As such, I've long considered this the suit most concerned with the area of life you're most passionate about. For me, fire is my relationship with my queerplatonic partner, and it is the theatre company we run. My fire is working with LGBTQQIP2SA+ tarot clients, and certainly in the written word. It's also about making this world so, so much better than I found it.

As you can see, Wands often indicate our careers, our families, or a hobby that we've chosen to never monetize for sheer love of it. For some it's their intuition, spirituality, or even life for its own sake. When originally queering the Wands, one of the biggest things I noticed was that often the thing a queer seeker is most passionate about is their queer identity itself. It took so long to find, live, and grow as yourself that your own queerness has become a brilliant bonfire that attracts only the best to sit within its light. Beyond that, though, it is a strange but wonderful fact that most queer people find themselves in activist or advocacy roles in their life, and that's where the true fire rages. Our identities and our right to live and express them are the things we find ourselves fighting for with unmatched fervor and commitment. Over time that fervor becomes about all of us, not just ourselves or our loved ones. Queer activism keeps us tirelessly fighting. Queer community is where we fall when we do get tired. These are the things we work through our fatigue to build and protect. These are the things we work ceaselessly to ensure that all queer people who come after us have. There are no words for the way many queer people approach their life as accidental activists except the ones we ascribe to the Wands: determination, fire, and passion.

One note before we move on: there are a lot of readers, books, and other resources that do address sex and gender in a generally progressive and LGBTQQ-IP2SA+ inclusive way. That's great, and obviously something I want to see way more of. However, I have seen Wands default to penis due to the phallic nature of many common depictions (and many literary metaphors used over time). While this is absolutely valid in some cases, I have seen that be wildly unhelpful to some of my clients. It can also be a trans exclusive interpretation if you're not careful. When queering the tarot, or hell, just talking to people out in the world and being decent, it's perfectly acceptable to talk about anatomy. But there are people who are not men who have penises, and people who are men who do not have penises. Understanding and keeping this in mind when you talk about the role anatomy does or does not play in the situation is crucial. For example, don't assume if you tell someone, based on the cards, that the partner with the penis is more trustworthy that it is referring to a male partner. The potential partner in question could be a trans woman, they could be non-binary, they could be intersex, and that's just to start. Really, if people take one thing away from this book or need a single starting point for becoming a reader who is accessible to LGBTQQIP2SA+ seekers, it should be this: never assume someone's gender, pronouns, or sexual identity, and always ask respectful, relevant questions if any of it comes up in a reading.

THE ACE OF WANDS

The Aces bring unexpected news into our lives. This can include insight you need, news from a third party, or a tangible item that shifts how you do your work. In Wands, that likely means news related to whatever it is you're most passionate about. I have seen news related to the job, partner, or spiritual path that you devote much of your energy to come up. I've also seen this card represent new ideas, a burst of creativity, or a fit of intuition that powers you through a tough decision.

Knowing our specific queer applications of the Wands brings a logical conclusion to queering the Ace: news related to our queer activism or community is coming. This can be anything from new hangouts cropping up that are safe for your chosen queer family, to that endless work of marching and letter writing coming to fruition. The Ace of Wands is when an important piece of legislation moves through, a community removes a barrier, or new words are added to the dictionary that validate those of us who felt invisible.

A queer Ace of Wands can come out very literally as well. If you're deciding between two partners, this card tells you to go where the passion and attraction are. While this isn't specific to LGBTQQIP2SA+ seekers, issues of attraction do come up often for those clients (and myself). Wands are very much about sex and spark, so acting on that will serve you well. This card is welcome permission to follow your groin. For polyam seekers, that means the Ace of Wands is often a new relationship or sexual encounter, likely not connected to anyone in your current poly circle. On this track of literalism, though, I've seen Aces indicate something else entirely regarding relationships: asexuality. While the Wands frequently bring up sex and lust, the Ace of Wands reversed or surrounded by cards affirming an asexual interpretation is likely leading us to that conclusion.

While the Ace of Wands can be great news for polyam people, if someone is questioning if they may be polyam or not in the first place, an Ace is a likely "No." Aces are a One, and sometimes the literal interpretation is the one we're looking for. This is especially true for the Ace of Wands. All of the wands, as mentioned, have a fiery, passionate, and therefore primal, carnal nature—but if you're regularly getting just a One when questioning your relationship orientation, you are probably not ready for a polyamorous relationship and are likely monogamous by nature. This idea of focusing on Ace as One also stretches into those questioning their sexual identity. While many of us have a very firm grip on who we are sexually and romantically, a lot of younger or newly out seekers (or seekers who are not out at all) will come to me asking if I can help give them insight into their sexual identity. Most of the wands would indicate non-monosexuality, but the Ace likely indicates that you are attracted to one gender.

The Ace of Wands does deal with sex and gender, as we've seen, but most often it is about a fire for life or for that area of life that brings our true passion to the surface. While we talk about our advocacy work as queer people as tireless, we know that's not true. We get exhausted. We get hurt. We don't win every battle, and too many losses in a row dampen our spirit. Then we're tired of fighting, and so often we're tired of *who we are* becoming a political statement even when we need a break from that world. It is then that Ace of Wands shows up promising us renewed vigor to get us through that last leg. The Ace of Wands is, in these times, a burst of inspiration that lights the way to the finish line that was once hidden from view. The Ace of Wands doesn't promise us that our spark will never burn out, but it does promise us that every time we burn out, our torch will be re-lit in time. This is a message that queer people need in a world that wants us to either keep fighting or stop existing, and in communities that mean well but don't always assess the frailty of human bodies and spirits before pulling us all in. This is a message of fire. It is news regarding fire. It is new fire. But in the case of this Ace, it's also a message of hope that shows up just when we start wondering if all this fire is even worth it.

THE TWO, THREE, AND FOUR OF WANDS

I mentioned that a lot of the Minor Arcana (a.k.a. the *suits* or *pips*) are really quick, straightforward cards. As such, to queer these cards it's sometimes easier to look at the overall picture than the individual pieces. The Two, Three, and Four of Wands are, of course, read individually within readings, but it's important to know where they fall in that suit's story, too. The beginner's understanding of the Two of Wands frequently indicates a business or creative partnership, and usually indicates long-term planning in whatever area of your life you're most passionate about. It can have a restless energy, as frequently we want the big prize of our long-term goals *now*, but it is also indicative that we are on the right track. Following this, the Three of Wands is about preparation and expansion. If someone asks about business and gets a Two, it's time to plan for the future, but from where you are now. The Three, then, is time to actually enact plans for expansion while still looking at the big five- and ten-year goals. If asking about romance or family, the Two indicates positive partnerships and making sure you want the same things out of life, and the Three indicates that it may be time to take that first step toward the future together.

Group work is well aspected in Threes in general, and the Wands *very* often indicate creative pursuits. I generally read the wands as "whatever area of life you're most passionate about" unless the seeker asks about a specific area of life. The Four of Wands continues this narrative, and at its base is about celebration and harmony in the area being discussed. Marriage, new living spaces, and a general concept of moving forward are indicated. If the seeker is asking about business, a change of location or a promotion could be indicated here. If asking about romance, this is a strong indication that marriage or cohabitation are on the horizon. If already

partnered in such a way, purchasing a house or expanding the family could be highlighted.

When queering the Two, Three, and Four of Wands, one of the biggest new ideas or changes we might see is that the area of life we're most passionate about becomes queer activism. The Wands usually correspond with fire, and therefore passion. However, fire can also represent destruction and the burning down of what is there that's not serving us. In this case it's easy to translate the Two of Wands as coming up with a plan or idea to create change and possibly finding a partner in these endeavors. The Three would be about enacting those plans, and the Four, a time of moving on to an even bigger project. The Four in this narrative could also mean seeing your hard activist or advocacy work pay off in a significant way. This card came up a lot when activists were fighting for marriage equality, and I've also seen it come up in times when anti-bully advancements were being made, for example. The Four also showed up once in a reading I did for a querent who used to be really close to their grandparents but were cut off from communication when they came out. They continued to live as a queer person and activist, fighting the good fight, and out of the blue one day their grandparents saw them on the news, became overwhelmed with guilt and pride, and reached out to make things right.

Because group work and family are strong elements of these cards, polyamory and unique chosen family situations are positively aspected here. If someone discloses a polyam identity or relationship, the Three and Four are strong indicators that it's a good time to welcome in new partners or take the next steps forward. These cards often come up for newly out polyam couples as a simple "it's time" assurance. For someone who has been seeing multiple partners for longer, it's usually a sign that one of the partners is a good match to either be welcomed into a current living situation, or to take significant step with in some way. The Two is interesting in this setting, because if someone is polyam and asking about a new interest or relationship, sometimes a Two is literally *just two*. This can be an indication that taking on a new partner or welcoming someone new into the fold is a bad idea right now. That restless energy will have to be resolved some other way—perhaps with more casual sex or by putting more energy into your existing partnerships. I mentioned queer chosen family settings before (that may not be polyam as the relationships may not be romantic or sexual in nature), and the same interpretations can be applied in those units.

Further queerings of this card are pretty straightforward. Because of the fire and passion in these cards, casual sex, threesomes, and flings are all aspected well. New relationships are aspected well with the Two, and while queer relationships do not always follow the traditional trajectory, the Three can indicate enacting plans you had together or getting serious about the relationship, and the Four making a significant move forward. There are, of course, a plethora of queer artists doing great work in the world and the Wands can be creative in nature, so these three cards are a sure sign that your current projects will succeed. The Two is finding a great collaborator, the Three is making plans, and the Four is successfully moving the project out to be seen by others.

The Wands are very big on communication. I joke about "queer lady processing" quite a bit, but it is a thing, and these three are pretty positive cards regarding that. Any hard conversations coming up are sure to go the best way possible with the Two, Three, or Four of Wands. If there are no big talks on the horizon, it may be time when the Two comes up to make you think about what you want that you're not on track for. When the Three shows up, it may be time to actually have the conversation and begin communicating with another as you plan your life from here on out. If it's the Four of Wands showing up in a suit of communication, it's time to start enacting the resolutions (or expected resolutions) from those hard conversations.

THE FIVE AND SEVEN OF WANDS

Conflict, competition, and conviction take center stage with these strife-filled Wands cards. While their interpretations do have differences, their similarities are plentiful and the way we queer them works together and includes a progression of the suit, not just a fresh take. Most often the Five of Wands very simply indicates conflict and tension. A straightforward reading sees familial conflicts that we get sucked into (especially as it follows the Four, which often indicates family), work meetings that may hit a heated head, or internal conflict between what our ideal self wants and actions we felt pressured into taking. As advice, this card may be telling you to back down, or it may be warning you to brace yourself. The tension is there, the conflict is coming, and the strife is a tangible thing you can at least name.

The Seven is similar, but has often manifested for myself and my clients as a time when it seems conflicts are running high (from multiple directions at that) and everything is coming at you at once. Notice I said this is how it *seems*—with the Seven, things could be blown out of proportion in your mind. You're well prepared to handle each blow as it comes, and are very likely to win any arguments headed your way.

Either card can indicate competition. To differentiate, I usually read the Five as a competition you're not quite ready for and the Seven as one that you are. Both cards also indicate conviction, although, again, there's much more strife in the Five so you may not be wholly satisfied by sticking to your conviction alone. It may be time to cool your jets and think about compromise, or it may be a time when you merely know you won't win this argument even if you're in the right. The Seven however promises a hard-fought, even-keeled sense of discourse where your cool head and conviction ultimately win out. With the Seven you want to fight tooth and nail to stand up for yourself, but there might be some other factors at play with the Five.

As we queer these cards, the unpleasantness continues, and at times the stakes are even higher for LGBTQQIP2SA+ querents. They could flat out indicate a strong amount of queerphobia in your family, at work, or in your professional field overall. With the Five, this may be a situation that seemed unpleasant but manageable at first, but has now gotten under your skin. As a reader I would likely advise you to put up boundaries if it is a family situation, or to seek employment elsewhere. You don't want this situation to grow into an untamable thing, and the best course (since no compromise can be reached here) is to make your exit.

The Seven, however, indicates that same sense of queerphobia affecting your family or work life except that, instead of leaving, you would be called to stand your ground and fight to make change from where you are. So even though the cards present similar themes and situations, they come with wildly different paths to take. In a reading, these most often show up if asked a yes or no-ish question like "Is my family really okay with this?"; "If I move in with my partner how will my family feel?"; or "Am I emotionally and career-wise safe at work if I take this next step in my transition?" The Five says, "No, the people involved in the situation will not be okay with this. It is likely you will need to put up boundaries, find a new employment situation first, or expect to feel alone for a little while." The Seven says, "Yes, things will be okay with time though it will take some fight, action, and conviction on your end."

A lower-stakes version comes when people ask about their queer family or ongoing conflicts there. While competition and conflict happen in any social circle, this can often feel amplified to queer people who already lack a solid social structure, so all of that Wands fire and energy can apply socially. Based on what we already know about these cards, the interpretation is pretty straightforward: if the queer chosen family or social circle is asked about or otherwise comes up in the reading, the Five indicates tension that may not have a resolution. Often this will blow over with time since there's not a fundamental refusal to accept you as you are, but it might be rough for a while, and you might have to be the one to bow out of the argument, lead a compromise, or enforce boundaries. The Seven though indicates that you are very likely in the right. If you stand your ground but also give other parties some space, you will come to the resolution you were hoping for.

The Wands are often that driving, fiery, energetic force in our life. They are why we get up in the morning and keep going. For LGBTQQIP2SA+ seekers, that is so often a person's queer identity itself or the activism and advocacy they have chosen to take on as a result of that identity. This idea of social justice or really *living in your identity* brings up some unique interpretations with the Five and Seven of Wands. In the very practical, the Five could be indicating that the campaign or project you're working on will create a lot of attention and controversy, but may not end with the desired political changes. The Seven would indicate the opposite. Getting your issue noticed and brought to light may be difficult, but ultimately the change you are seeking will occur.

One way I've really seen the Five, in particular, play out is when someone's identity itself *is* their passion, but then their identity starts shifting. If you brand your solo entrepreneurship as being for lesbians, trans men, or asexual clients, for example, and then your own identity starts shifting, the Five is likely to indicate that internal conflict is really throwing you for a loop. The Seven would show you that you have a lot of loyal clients and audience and though it could be difficult to rebrand, it can be done. The Five shows you may have a harder go of it, but to resolve that tension you do need to think of a solution. This card alone may not tell you what possible solutions are, but neighboring cards may. While that's an example with money and business on the line, the same concepts apply if you've built your non-business life around your identity and it begins shifting.

What I always come back to when I'm queering the Five and Seven of Wands is the need to look at them as a progression. Often that Five shows up in the past or present, indicating a time where pain or disagreements cloud the querent's thinking, making them unable to keep a cool head or find a place of peace within. The Seven always comes later though—at a time when we are at the top of our game, can embrace competition or hate as a conquerable part of life, and when our strength and righteousness win out.

Each Five of Wands period in our life is meant to lead us to a place of the Seven of Wands, and each conflict only makes us stronger. These are rough cards when you're in the middle of them, but they do make us better if we let them. With the Five we learn the art of compromise. We learn when to pick our battles, and that's an unfortunate part of LGBTQQIP2SA+ life, too. Not every ignorant prejudiced jerk can be educated, and if they're close to us in emotional intimacy or proximity that's a tough pill to swallow. But ultimately that knowledge prepares us for the battles that truly matter—those represented in the Seven that crack open hearts and minds, allowing passion and raw human instinct and need for love to supersede all, and those that show us how strong we've become without even realizing it.

THE SIX AND EIGHT OF WANDS

The most common keywords for the Six are progress, victory, and triumph. When I hear the words victory and triumph though, I don't just think of the success or win that comes with them. These words bring battle, rough terrain, and hard-fought success to my mind, and that's important to note for this card. This isn't just a good thing happening—it's something you've fought long and hard for finally turning in your favor. It's triumph over adversity, specifically.

The Eight is associated with progress too, although much more speedily. It's not that you *haven't* been working tirelessly for the win that comes in the Eight, it's that there's no steady or slow growth. Things aren't going in your favor, or they've stagnated, and then all of a sudden, *BOOM*. Quick action, quick decisions on your part, and quick changes to the energy surrounding a situation bring this triumph.

Because a queer perspective of the Wands suit is often connected to the passion for social justice many queer people share, we'll start with the obvious to queer these two cards.

Social justice is *hard*—fighting for our own rights and sticking up for marginalized groups we're allied with seems overwhelming and insurmountable more often than not. These cards bring welcome news to our activist lives, with the Six promising that a rough campaign or project will succeed, while the Eight most often brings a fresh burst of energy to an ongoing battle, allowing you to push through the last bit of work and turn the tide. In short, both promise victories over oppression, particularly if you've been fighting for a specific piece of liberation or legislation.

However, many believe that social justice and the key to equality or liberation (depending on your goals) start with the deeply personal. As such, I have seen the Six of Wands show up when someone's transphobic or otherwise bigoted relative realizes they've been wrong to isolate a queer seeker or continue to push a harmful political or personal agenda on them. A joyful, earnest conversation or show of support from such a loved one certainly did not come easy. It came after years of arguments and in-depth conversation. I have seen the Eight do the opposite—seekers who get this card are promised a sudden burst of passionate advocacy from others. This is likely when the seeker decides to move on beyond those who have hurt them and stumbles into a queer chosen family almost by accident. Finding your people always amounts to a flurry of emotion and activity, and this is often what this Eight of Wands indicates.

When we talk about the deeply personal, though, we are not just talking about how the oppression marginalized people face shows up in close interpersonal relationships. It's most important to look at how it shows up within *ourselves*. We hear about internalized misogyny and internalized homophobia all the time, and I know for a fact that other *isms* and hatred also get turned within. This is something LGBTQQIP2SA+ seekers deal with so often that we almost dismiss that part of our story and our struggle—the part where everything is going right but we still feel wrong or fight who we are. The number one way I see the Six of Wands show up is when an LGBTQQIP2SA+ querent finally begins accepting and embracing their queerness, instead of just going through the motions of living it. And, as with stumbling into a queer squad of our own, this can often happen quickly, following a series of chance encounters with supportive people or life itself quickly doing a one-eighty and showering us with generosity. This is when the Eight of Wands shows up. The Eight would also come up in instances where we're still working to truly embrace our full selves, perhaps suggesting we follow our gut into a series of self discovery-provoking events that help us fall in love with ourselves all over again.

In the mundane, the Six and Eight of Wands don't necessarily warrant queer-ing—victory or action and quick changes in our jobs, relationships, diets, and so on, are still just that. When we look at these cards through a queer lens though, we see something else entirely—victory against societal ick, activity and gain in our personal lives, and eventually, triumph over those parts of ourselves that don't actually want us to triumph.

THE NINE OF WANDS

I originally wrote about the Nine of Wands shortly after the 2016 American election that devastated so many in our community. It was comforting and reinvigorating to me to be writing about the Nine of Wands then, and as a response to the drain and stress so many of us feel right now, this card deserves its own standalone piece. However, this card deals a lot with negative cycles, and two years into a cycle filled with the ugliest parts of humanity in my country, I am feeling frustrated again, even as I work on this generally hopeful book. I am also feeling terrified, anxious, and stressed out daily because of what the past couple of years have looked like for queer people, POC, the disabled, women, and other marginalized people.

Yet I know that the Wands are a suit full of ups and downs and filled with conflict. I also know that very often the suit indicates that a resolution of those conflicts is coming. It's a suit that shows up to represent our gut instinct and that source of intuition, and is heavy on communication and creativity. It's also the suit that correlates with fire and, as such, represents all of those things that make life worth living: sex, intensity, and the things we personally are most passionate about. We've been talking about how, for queer people, those passions lie in queer activism and even our very identities. We've discussed how those affect the personal in the Two through Four, the hard activist fights of the Five and Seven, and the joyous triumphs of the Six and Eight. I also know that the Nine of Wands is tied to keywords like persistence, bravery, tenacity, and even the phrase "test of faith." It represents those moments when we've come through hell and all of a sudden it feels . . . pointless. There's been a setback of any size, and that hard work we've been putting in seems to dissipate right before our eyes.

It is a frustrating card to get in a prophetic placement, because it says, "Oh, hey, a speed bump is coming and it's a big one." But it's a great card to get elsewhere, because it shows how far you've come, and it promises that though this may feel like your toughest battle yet, it's not the war itself, and the war itself is winnable. In fact, you've actually already won the battle in question. It's just a matter of sticking it out and pushing through, allowing yourself to admit you've grown exponentially from previous experiences, and this time, you're ready. This is a card that idealizes standing up for your beliefs, and so it often shows up simply to tell us the fight is worth it. It's a card of resilience. It's a card of resistance. As advice, the Nine of Wands is almost tough love, telling us to just *be* resilient—to resist. Letting someone or something else win at this point is nonsense. Keep going. It's necessary to hold on to the message of this card, as hard as it may be and as angry or hurt as you may be. It doesn't take much imagination to apply the above to our current struggles for queer equity and liberation.

In case you need to straight up hear it anyway: the fight for LGBTQQIP2SA+ rights isn't over. We have been dealt a harsh blow, but the progress we have made over the past decade isn't disappearing, at least not right now. We are stronger and better as individuals and as a community, and we will continue to fight to protect our existing rights and push for the plethora of rights and dignities we still do not have. This would be true if the Nine of Wands showed up in a reading, but it's also a card that wants to hold our attention all the time. These lessons translate to our own microcosms too, as many of us feel down after dealing with racist or queerphobic family. The Nine of Wands tells you to keep working with your family (or whoever is causing the pain), and going with those conversations and that hyperpersonal activism. If you take nothing else away from this book, take that—*keep going.* But take this too: you are strong enough to do so.

While I am speaking directly to current events and issues, the same queering I've talked about can apply anytime, in any year or month that the Nine of Wands shows up for you, about any setback or struggle on your path of advocacy or even when fighting to be heard in your family or personal life. It's also true for the internal conflicts that the suit of Wands seeks to address. The LGBTQQIP2SA+ community is imbued pretty deeply with issues of mental health, sobriety, and self-worth for understandable reasons. We are marginalized people, and we're going to have some reactions to that. As we think about taking control of ourselves, and taking our lives back from even internal sources, the Nine of Wands shows up to confirm that we've got this. Maybe we didn't a year or two or seven ago, but here in this moment, a temporary self-esteem slip or return to self-destructive behavior isn't going to throw us totally off course. This card shows up to say that in this moment, we are able to pull ourselves up and continue on our path of healing.

The Nine of Wands can apply to slightly lighter situations too. If your identity has fallen more into questioning than any firm letter in even the expanded acronym, or if you are fairly fluid, you are reaching a point where those cases of fluidity no longer throw you off track or make you question everything about who you are. Though it's always a little strange to find yourself feeling or identifying outside of your wheelhouse, the Nine of Wands shows that you can still retain your sense of self as you either wade through this new territory or begin incorporating it into your life.

The Nine of Wands can show up in our personal or romantic lives, too. We are all sometimes tempted off track by a cute femme just slightly too young for us who doesn't want the same things out of life but sure is sweet when she shows up at your work with coffee. (Okay, maybe this is a really specific piece of personal testimony, but we all have those weaknesses, whether it's a specific ex, type of relationship, or, yes, type of person). If the Nine of Wands shows up in a future placement, this is a warning to hold on to your hat because that situation is likely arising soon. In this and any other placement, this card also reminds us of how far we've come in our personal growth since our last merry-go-round. As a Wands card (which does prioritize passion and therefore sometimes carnal desires), in this type of reading the message may not be to stand your ground and say no no matter what. Rather, it's saying if we choose to walk through the flames this time, and there are times when we just really need our flames nurtured, it will not crush us when it inevitably falls apart or when we have to be the ones to pull the plug. Don't lose sight of who you are in the process, or in the aftermath, and your personal and domestic goals will still be met on time with your self-worth intact. There are times when the Wands firmly say to stand up to the person and refuse relationships that are actually unhealthy, or when we know we aren't sexually compatible with someone, for example. But there is an alternate way to read this card, and that does include embracing our sexual side.

As we move forward in this new world, we are wrapping up a lot of terrifying battles. Some we've even won. Many more were unfortunately lost. I'm going to break from format a little by ending with a suggestion for a reading to guide whatever is hurting your queer heart right now. If you read, great, if not, find a friend or professional who does, and ask for this:

- First, pull the Nine of Wands out, and let it oversee the whole reading. Think about the things that have you feeling defeated, be they personal or societal.

- Lay out three more cards in any order. These are steps you can take to put this time behind you and feel triumphant by year's end.

- Pull one more card as a final message, and let that message be your mantra over the next six to eight weeks. If it's Death, for example, the mantra would be "Everything that ends makes room for something new," or if it's something like the Five of Wands, it's a basic reminder that walking away from what's causing you pain is an option right now.

The Nine of Wands promises we're ready to start anew—it's just a matter of planting our feet, summoning our strength, and looking ahead (which many of us admittedly haven't been great at lately). The number one message of the Nine of Wands is a defiant, confident "You got this," and I can't think about a stronger, more important message for marginalized communities to receive right now.

THE TEN OF WANDS

Oh, friends, if there's ever a time to assess the Ten of Wands in all of its potential queer glory, it's now. The past few years have been completely overwhelming and exhausting regardless of where you land on the political or social spectrum. For many of us concerned with collective liberation and freedom, each New Year hasn't exactly reset things the way we hoped. As a result, many of us are running around trying to fix it all at once, feeling defeated and losing steam every step of the way. Appropriately then, the Ten of Wands is a card of complete and utter exhaustion. It indicates burnout; it indicates feeling burdened; and it indicates that if you aren't there now, you are about to fall apart if one more thing lands on your plate.

This is also a card warning us that no matter what our intentions were going into a situation, we are now knee-deep in unfair or codependent burdens that shouldn't belong to us in the first place. As a person, this is someone who either takes on others' problems as their own or who expects others to do that for them. As an event, this is the moment you're just *done* with a situation that has been ordeal after ordeal. You have officially reached burnout. As advice, this card lets us know it is time to take a huge step back from such a person or situation and take a long, deep look at the habits that regularly put us here.

Queering the Ten of Wands is somewhat uncomfortable for me as so much of my work on this series is geared toward building up community and building up individual LGBTQQIP2SA+ seekers. Sometimes, though, to become empowered, we have to reach a dark rock bottom first. And sometimes we have to acknowledge that for all of our radical power, we too are human and flawed. Queering the Ten of Wands often means addressing the frequently codependent need to fix everything for fellow queer people and our penchant for working too hard in relationships that we know aren't worth it, and acknowledging that we are prone to take on as many activist, advocate, and community roles as we think we can handle without much thought to our basic human needs like sleep and proper meals.

I see this card come up disproportionately with queer seekers because we are so on fire to create change that we often cannot see we are headed into dangerous territory. You can't give thirsty people water when your own cup is empty, and I see so many cases of overload where every card I lay out is about self-care and adequate rest when reading for my community. When the Ten of Wands shows up you have to take a step back, no matter how much you love your projects, or you will end up so frazzled and spent you will be unable to help anyone, including yourself. This card often addresses compassion fatigue, a type of anxiety faced by those who do a lot of helping work and community organizing that comes from taking on all of the problems you're trying to resolve as your own. It's exhausting to be someone who gives a damn about marginalized people, let alone the fact that that involvement often reinforces the trauma that comes from being marginalized oneself. This means facing the hard realities of putting up boundaries when we really don't want to, and having to shut off part of our empathy to the very real suffering those we care about are facing so that we can continue to do the hard work of creating change and offering direct support to those who need it.

Finally on this note, while a codependent need to take on a partner's problems as our own is by far not a specifically LGBTQQIP2SA+ phenomenon, it does manifest a little differently and a little more often. I mentioned before how taking on someone else's trauma can reinforce our own, and that's certainly true in these cases as well. I want to emphasize that most people who get the Ten of Wands in situations like this are compassionate people in positive relationships. The problems are that we haven't learned to put up emotional and spiritual boundaries to protect ourselves, and that we've been so focused on these other problems that technically aren't even ours that we have abandoned our own needs. In short, this card often shows a problem that exists in us, not the other people involved. When this card shows up over and over again, it can mean we've developed a habit of taking on other people's issues as our own, and its appearance requires self-assessment and honesty to figure out why that's happening and how we can prevent it in the future. The Ten of Wands wants us to figure out how we can start healing that part of us that chooses to do that. How this shows up uniquely for LGBTQQIP2SA+ people is that the need at hand comes from a place where we identify with the problem or pain, and think subconsciously, for example, that if we somehow fix a close friend's relationship with their transphobic parent, our own tenuous relationship with casually homophobic high school friends will somehow also reach a peaceable conclusion. This causes us to focus on these other problems instead of our own, but we also take on so many that it inevitably leads here, to the Ten of Wands, to a place of feeling broken, not better.

The of Ten of Wands can also show up to represent the radical collective or queer community as a whole when a traumatic event happens that takes the wind out of our normally energetic sails. This is when a querent is generally good about boundaries and self-care but something unprecedented happens that just knocks us completely off our feet. The 2016 American presidential election and everything that has happened after are perfect examples. Each innocent black person murdered by police is another example. The shooting at Pulse nightclub in 2016 is yet another. In these times we think the solution is to immediately hop back up and into action. We deprive ourselves of the time to grieve, but in the end, the human need to rest and mourn always wins. It's okay to feel defeated, and though the Ten of Wands often shows up to give us advice or steer us a certain way, in these cases it shows up to say, "I hear you. I see you. I love you. Please give yourself the same love I am giving you."

You do not want that beautiful Wands fire to turn into rage, and you do not want it to sizzle out completely. There are times that require action (like the Eight of Wands), and times that do not. Now your job is not to act. It is to feel your pain fully, to give in to your exhaustion, and to take even a few moments or (preferably) days to rest your weary, broken heart. It is in that rest that the fire reignites, and we can cycle back around to the beginning of this suit. If Wands are about fire and action and Tens are about transformation, we have to remember that the transformation at the end of a fiery run is born out of ashes, not new fires. Many think of the Wands suit, especially at the end, as a wildfire, and that metaphor certainly has merit. But it can also be likened to the Phoenix, and if you want to rise again and cycle back to that Ace, you have to sink fully into the ashes of defeat first.

3

THE SUIT OF SWORDS

The Swords are our suit of logic, mental clarity, and intellect, but these cards often bring sudden bad news. The Swords' purpose is to force us to cut away the things in our life that aren't working (even if we really, really like those things), so we can continue growing instead of standing still. The Swords do not always bring us what we want, but they do get us what we need. This is the suit that corresponds with Air, so it is a suit of swift-moving action, where clear thought and precise actions are needed to reach our goals.

As we queer the Swords, one of the big things I want to look at is how mental illness, sobriety, and identity intersect in the LGBTQQIP2SA+ community. Because this suit can indicate mental illness for *anyone*, ignoring that life on the margins causes unique manifestations of mental illness or that medical care for queer people is disgustingly inadequate in a lot of places would be ridiculous and irresponsible. The queer community has a long history of alcoholism that many believe stems from the fact that we used to be able to meet other queer people only in illicit and underground bars. The queer community has an even longer history of being denied adequate mental health and medical care. Our needs are not the same as someone who has no experience with queerness. There's a specific psychology and specific sexual health education that all queer people need that I have yet to find a satisfying version of. There are certainly transgender-specific health care needs, and while there are doctors who specialize in this, they are few. It is still too difficult and too rare for a trans person to be able to access the help they need. That means any mental illness or addiction that creeps in goes untreated indefinitely, creating very unique-to-our-community manifestations of the Swords cards.

Beyond health, mental health, and addiction, bigger issues of justice also prevail in the Sword cards. This suit is very invested in right and wrong, moving forward or staying stuck, and what our spiritual self wants versus our Earthbound self. Because the word and concept of justice are such a tense topic in the LGBTQQIP2SA+ (and really any marginalized) community, and because by nature the Swords suit is more negative, many of the cards represent hard decisions where we lose no matter what we choose and often show events or people that are negative or hurtful. However, the Swords suit often calls you to pick up the sword and fight for your version of justice. This often means with actual fighting, and though that's often best left to the Wands suit, here it frequently means with words and cunning instead. The Swords also represent intellect and writing, and even my least spiritual clients often connect well to this suit's straightforward news and insights.

THE ACE OF SWORDS

The Ace of Swords usually brings swift, sudden news that can anger you or break your heart, and it's not news my clients like to receive. This is one of the cards that shows up if we're expecting illness or injury, and it's one that can predict heartbreak with pretty good accuracy. It does have some positive incarnations though. Swords are a logical suit, and frequently a sudden, brash insight will rock our world in the best way possible. This is news that cuts away things we've wanted to be rid of, or suddenly reveals how to solve that pesky problem that's been nagging us for months. The

tarot almost always wants to push you to your highest and best self, and this card's ultimate purpose is to remove the things that are unnecessary in your life. So, while many times this is a maligned card, even the unexpected bad news is meant to rid us of whatever prevents us from being our best selves. You may have loved that partner, but they weren't right for you. The loss in your family might be great, but the person was sick for a while and was ready to go. These may be hard realities to face, but they ultimately lead us to where we need to go.

One of the first ways we queer this Ace is simply by taking all of that into account and applying it explicitly to queer people. I have seen this card manifest for me, personally, as warning that a depressive spell, panic attack, or other signifier of mental illness is imminent. This has also been true for LGBTQQIP2SA+ seekers living in sobriety, although in this case it can indicate an actual relapse or desire for one on the horizon. This is another way that queering the tarot does deconstruct it a bit. Obviously these things are not meant to lead us to our higher self. They are battles that we face regularly, though, and this Ace shows up almost daring us to let this side of ourselves win. The bad news is not meant to help us grow, but the way we fight against these relapses is.

The flip side of this iteration of the Ace is for those who have been struggling with mental illness or who know their drinking or drug use is becoming a problem. In these cases, the Ace of Swords promises a breakthrough—an ability to quit, a change in mood for the better, or a life-changing moment in therapy, for example. There can also be and often is a sense of victory in this card, and for LGBTQQIP2SA+ querents, that breakthrough usually comes with a promise that the resources and community you need to navigate your addiction or mental illness are right at your fingertips. So many people don't get sober because they don't know of a queer sober community near them, or because they don't know where to seek treatment in a place that won't other or misgender them. With the Ace, the need to prioritize your health looms large, but it's followed by the promise that there is a queer rehab center or Narcotics Anonymous group near you.

The Ace of Swords as the bearer of bad news can be especially cruel to LGBTQQ-IP2SA+ querents. I never rule out someone outing a seeker without permission or someone being confronted or treated with hostility because of their identity when this card shows up. There are experiences you can't understand unless you yourself are queer, and the callousness of someone outing us without permission and putting us in danger is one of them. That is a very real manifestation of this Ace, and I don't want to spin or belittle that.

However, when we think about queering the tarot, we think about subversion. While this card is always hard, it could be telling you to take matters into your own hands. This could be a clear message that now is the time for *you* to deliver news about your identity, transition, or life to others who may not want to hear it. While there are always repercussions, oftentimes tragic ones, if the Ace shows up to push you this way, it's because, quite simply, it's your time to do so. If it gets to this point, you've probably been waiting too long and fate (or whatever your concept of that is) is about to intervene if you don't take action yourself. Often we are asked to wield the sword, deliver the hard blow, and whatever falls away as a result needed to so that you can walk through life as your fabulous queer self unencumbered by the burden of secrets or those who will refuse to love you as a result of them. It is a hard card because it cuts away the strings that keep us tied, but it is a necessary card because (unlike some other Swords we'll explore in a bit) this card shows this is not the time for us to be bound.

Tied to this idea, I've also seen the Ace of Swords show up for transgender clients who are thinking about gender-affirming surgeries. In this case the idea of cutting away the unnecessary becomes very literal, and the message that it's time can come as a welcome relief even if there are a lot of logistics to figure out. Swords cards love logistics even when we don't. In these cases, this card is a promise that it's time to take that leap and that you'll be thrilled with the results if you do. You'll feel free from a life you've been trying to kill off for a long time. This suit does correspond with Air, and with that come images of birds flying and butterflies transforming, and I can think of no better message to leave any client with, but especially one who has been facing gender dysphoria and external oppression at every turn.

Then there's the saucier side of the Ace of Swords. This card has a very dominant energy that can be applied sexually, especially regarding BDSM or other kink. An optional interpretation if you're reading for a querent who's strongly kink-identified is a quick note from the cards that it's time to escalate your play or learn a new format for training and punishment. I've seen this card literally manifest as knife play, for example, but often it's just time to learn to tie some new knots or implement a new tool for impact play. In any case, taking action and control over your sex life is an incredibly mood-shifting idea for most LGBTQQIP2SA+ people who grew up in repressed households, which, quite frankly, was most of us. This Sword wants you to grab it, and be safe, but jump into, ahem, action expressing your queer self carnally. As such it can cut away the ties to monogamy that don't fit many of us, as well as push us toward kink. If you're reading about your sex life, the bottom line is this: take control.

The queerly dominant energy of the Ace of Swords goes back to the idea that you are being called on to bear news others may perceive as bad—breaking up with a partner that loves you, coming out in a space where others will respond poorly, or being your own sword-bearer and going to rehab or into therapy. It's a card that cuts away what isn't working in your life, and what doesn't suit most LGBTQQIP2SA+ seekers is letting someone or something else call the shots in our life, whether that something is alcohol or drugs, our assigned bodies, or whatever else is holding us back. What I stated above stands for LGBTQQIP2SA+ querents regardless—when the Ace of Swords shows up, it's time for you to take control. It might show up as bad news or be heavy with the weight of other people's expectations, but that's not for you to focus on. You are fully equipped to pick up this Sword and forge a clear path to your highest, queerest, sexiest self, and the Ace of Swords wants to see you through until the very end.

THE TWO, THREE, AND FOUR OF SWORDS

The Two, Three, and Four of Swords make more sense if we queer them as a group and look at the narrative, similar to the approach we took with the Wands. While these three cards are thematically opposed, there's a clear message of mental clarity, heartbreak, and fallout in them. We start with the Two of Swords, a card that most often shows up in times of indecision due to the gravity of the choice at hand, or for situations where we've exhausted our options and are at a stalemate. In either case, our judgment becomes clouded and we feel blind to options and ways out. I have a deck that has colored how I see this card, where the Two regularly indicates that you know exactly what you're meant to do now, but doing so requires a leap of faith and insists that you not use that famous Swords logic to its full extent.

This card interestingly gives way to the Three of Swords, one of the most feared but important cards in the deck. Its most commonly used keyword is simply heartbreak. As this card follows the Two, I often see it as the result of what happens when you take a leap of faith. Either you're called to take the leap and it doesn't work out, or taking the leap requires sacrifices and emotional processing you didn't expect. Alternatively, if the Two means we're at a stalemate in a relationship or business situation, the Three sees us leaving that in a way that is devastating, even if it is for the best. This leads us to the Four of Swords, a card of rest, meditation, and recuperation. After the action-packed time that the Two leads us into and the emotional exhaustion of the Three, the Four calls us to take care of ourselves, putting our bodies at rest and clearing our minds for a bit.

As an LGBTQQIP2SA+ person, this mini-suit within the Swords suit often tells a very frank coming out story. If we look at coming out as something that is not straight and cisgender, we start with feeling trapped in the decision of whether to do so or not. At some point our own logic and perspective become cloudy like they do in that Two. Eventually though, most of us have to make the decision to come out. That can, unfortunately, also lead to the sadness and despair of the Three. There are many cards you can throw down and see the coming out process, but the Three of Swords is one of the only cards that straightforwardly reminds us that sometimes we really do lose family and friends as part of that process. The response to that is the Four: time to rest and prioritize caring for ourselves since we are seemingly on our own in this next phase.

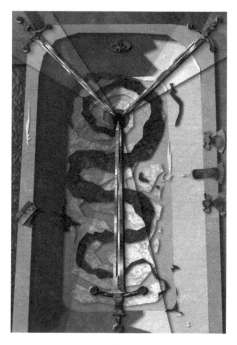

This same line of narrative can be applied to transgender people who are contemplating or beginning transitioning. There's the Two's indecision and lack of clarity—although in this case, that lack of clarity is often rooted in actual lack of knowledge on where to go for hormones, surgery, or undergarments. Frequently, though, it comes from not being sure when the right time to transition is, or wondering if the time will ever feel right. When the Two comes up, its third-party insight is likely meant to urge the querent forward in their transition. Once the trans querent has worked through the Two, we come to the Three. In this case though, the Swords can also be a metaphor for gender-affirming surgery or "going under the knife" for trans people. I've had a couple of clients that, when faced with a lot of Swords cards, made jokes like "Guess surgery's looking good?" and that is often the case with the Three. Heartbreak can be a metaphor for anything that's removed from our lives, and certainly surgical transition is not without its heartbreaks and sadnesses along the way. In both of these examples, the Four shows up to remind us that our bodies and our minds are incredibly important, even when we're more concerned with our hearts. So after all of that pain, get some sleep! Take introvert time, or hot showers, or whatever you need to

feel rested up. For those who are spiritually inclined, meditation is key here. If you're not spiritually inclined, finding a way to clear your mind instead of letting that negative fallout fester is crucial. Even if a trans person opts out of surgical transition (which many do), the transition process includes getting rid of pieces of the closeted version of yourself, be that clothes or even photos from your upbringing.

As the Swords can indicate concerns with mental health, and the LGBTQQ-IP2SA+ community deals with disproportionate amounts of mental illness, I would be remiss to not explore the Two through Four of Swords from a mental health standpoint. The Two of Swords indicates a time when we can't find our way back to center or to balance. It indicates not being able to make decisions or see clearly in a way that rings very true for those of us who struggle with anxiety. In this case, getting someone else's perspective or taking time to clear one's mind may not be the most helpful advice for a querent. Though this card often requires leaping first and looking later, if it's showing up in a placement or a way that screams "behavior" and not "advice," you're likely looking at someone who struggles with manic episodes common in bipolar disorder. In those situations, the guidance you'd see from a tarot reader should be very different and should caution one away from actually taking leaps of faith right now. The Three of Swords, however, is frequently a clear indication of severe depression cycling back to a very dark state. You can look at the Two and Three of Swords cards together and see a bipolar querent. You can look at them separately and see anxiety in the Two and depression in the Three. In either case, it's critical to remember that the seeker cannot control those cycles or those highs and lows. The cards can serve as very effective warnings to the seeker to look out for relapse, and can provide the reader more information about the very real obstacles facing the seeker. However, tarot readers are not therapists, and the advice that comes with these cards should include traditional approaches like therapy and medication to deal with these swings. The Swords deal with anything logical and analytical, and that does include traditional medicine. The Four of Swords largely encourages the querent to get back to resting and making time for themselves, although it can also indicate the exhaustion and burnout that living with mental illness can bring. That advice doesn't change, though: Rest. Clear your mind. Trust yourself.

Once we see how the Two, Three, and Four of Swords work together to take us from decision to heartbreak to rest, we can apply them to a number of other situations in a queer person's life. LGBTQQIP2SA+ relationships are a little bit more intense emotionally, both because our dating pool is thinner, and because we spend so long in the closet *not* honoring our emotions that there is a very real, valid need to pamper them a little bit extra when out. As such, this narrative applies to starting new queer relationships, ending those relationships, or joining queer-led social groups. The Two pushes us to do so, and then we're left more than a little hurt and surprised when it leads to that Three. It's important to remember that the heartbreak of the Three of Swords does not always come in the way we think it will. Sometimes relationships don't work out—but very often in the LGBTQQIP2SA+ community they do, yet it's a whole new level of hurt and oppression from other people that faces us once we're dating someone (or a number of someones). While this is primarily true for those whose sexual identity is queer, for transgender people it is still not uncommon for a close friend or family member to be accepting until they see you dating someone they don't expect.

A specialty of mine is reading tarot for healing purposes, particularly for those dealing with the aftermath of trauma. This line of work, like my identity-based tarot readings, attracts primarily LGBTQQIP2SA+ querents. There are a number of reasons for this, starting with the societal trauma of being othered in the first place, and reaching into the deeply personal. There is often a lack of resources specifically for or related to queer people who have been traumatized, and there's very often a concern about what society at large will think if word of abusive LGBTQQIP2SA+ people gets out. In these cases, pulling any one of these cards tells me more about where the querent is in terms of their own healing. Often with the Two, they are contemplating treatment, speaking out, or debating other common methods of healing. Their vision is compromised because of societal pressure, and because they have, quite frankly, probably never seen representation of lesbians being sexually assaulted, trans people being attacked, or dominant BDSM partners being abusive, which means they have no idea what to do or where to go for help. They don't know if speaking out will do any good. They have no idea what their next move should be.

Healing is personal, just like everything else, and the advice with the Two is that whatever you are scared of doing is probably the right thing for you to do right now. That could mean telling people what happened. That could mean pressing charges. It could also mean going to therapy to heal from the situation. The Three, alternatively, encourages those who have been traumatized to take a much gentler approach. "Let yourself be hurt, sad, angry," urges this card. Live in that misery. Stew in it. Be incredibly self-indulgent. Life is about cycles, and there is a time for everything, and that includes a time to sink down into the reality of what's happened and allow it to surround you. It is only in that encampment that you can use your logical mind to start cutting through all of the pain. The Four tells me the querent has already done quite a bit of healing work. Healing work, however, has the word *work* attached to it on purpose. It's exhausting to sit with your emotions and focus on your healing 24/7. At some point, you still need to rest. At some point, the only thing that's going to further your healing is taking time to recuperate. At some point, pain turns into straight up exhaustion, and that, too, is a feeling you should honor.

In any case, the Four rounds out this mini-narrative for a reason. After experiencing new or deepened pain or trauma, you need some *you* time, whatever that may look like. This is so often the message of the Swords overall. We get hurt, yet life goes on, and if you don't take the time to recuperate from the pain, it's going to keep bringing you back to a cycle of uncertainty and heartbreak over and over again. That's true for any querent, but in the LGBTQQIP2SA+ community, we are more likely to be working with additional disadvantages, dealing with mental health concerns, or finding ways unique to our queer experience that this plays out, such as coming out or starting a new relationship. Therefore it's even more important to understand the way these three cards are interpreted when we're learning whole suits at a time—if we don't know about the potential for heartbreak, we could stay stuck in the Two of Swords' place of confusion indefinitely. If we don't know about the importance of rest, that Three of Swords can be crushing.

Given that, my final piece of advice for getting one of these cards in a reading is to pull just one more card asking, "What's the best way for me to rest or take care of myself right now?" Like anything else, that answer can look wildly different depending on the person, but that final card can ease the concerns of anyone facing big, scary choices, staring down heartbreak, or feeling completely wiped out.

THE FIVE AND SEVEN OF SWORDS

We've reached two of the hardest cards to face in the tarot deck: The Five and Seven of Swords. These two represent oppression both large scale and personal. They represent pain, theft, and the feeling of drowning or being trapped in your misery. All Swords bear the cool, calculating motivation of justice, and the Five and Seven are warning you of incoming danger or reminding you of past trauma you aren't over yet because they want you to work through it in real time and end up on the other side. It will obviously hurt, though, and these cards are prime examples of painful times that we have to deal with in order to push past them and move on.

I've chosen to queer these two cards together because I tend to think of them as two different faces of oppression or trauma. The Five of Swords traditionally represents someone trying to hold you down and prevent you from moving forward or gaining an advantage. This card is arguments, hostility, and tension that build to an eventual action-filled climax. Except . . . it doesn't have to build to that climax. A lot of tarot card images show the presumed seeker walking away from the conflict or deciding this isn't theirs to deal with. There's usually a feeling of sadness in the walking away, as if the seeker at hand is sacrificing or giving up too much as they leave. However, as a queer person this idea leaves me with rays of hope. In a queer reading of this card, we are looking societal oppression pretty straight in the face. This is when we realize that as LGBTQQIP2SA+ people we will encounter individuals, institutions, even entire continents that will never embrace or accept us simply because of who we are. This card is the realization that we will always be fighting and we will still always be oppressed. Or . . . we could choose to walk away from the fight, develop a tight-knit chosen family in a progressive city, for example, and live fully in that. You and a partner could settle down in a cabin in the woods and just not deal with that outside hatred.

That might be surprising to hear me say when I've been talking so much about collectives and equity. The Five of Swords shows that none of those choices is wrong. You could become the strongest, toughest, most cutthroat activist there is. You could also decide, "Actually, a lot of this progress looks like assimilation. This isn't for me," or, "This is too hard, and I can't do it. Living my life is resistance enough," and step out of that fight. On a micro scale, not every activist is meant for every fight. Backing out this time doesn't mean you won't pick up a sword later, it simply means you can't justify fighting the good fight right now. That's 100 percent fine, and the Five of Swords wants to make us keenly aware of the full range of options ahead of us.

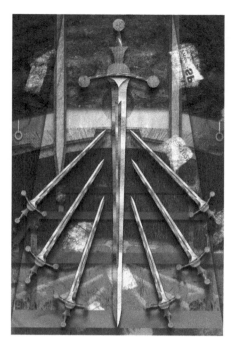

I briefly mentioned that in addition to oppression, the Five of Swords can also be about trauma. While I think the Three of Swords and the Seven of Swords hit on specific traumatic events as they happen to us as individuals, there is a real need to identify collective trauma in the tarot as well. If a sexual assault shows up as the Three or Seven of Swords, then the Five of Swords is the rape culture where that assault goes unreported or is not taken seriously. If the Three or Seven shows an abusive family, a hate crime, losing one's home, loved one, or something else important for racist or queerphobic reasons, the Five is the world where those one-off actions exist that fosters and nurtures the *isms* and hatred that make us unsafe and unsupported. Unfortunately, these are times when walking away may not be possible. Pull a few additional cards to see what the seeker's options are as they move forward in this time. If it still all comes back to this Five, it might be a call for the seeker to rest before jumping in for justice again or to seek out other survivors dealing with similar types of trauma. At the end of the day, this card still may be a call to move out of that oppressive situation, and whatever your reasons for staying, they may not be enough to justify feeling so trapped for so long.

If the Five of Swords represents oppressive and traumatic outside oppressors and shows us how to deal with them, the Seven of Swords, then, is individual theft, deception, or betrayal. It is someone or something that steals from you, although likely metaphorically. In other words, it is someone stealing energy, time, or pieces of your heart from you. (It is worth mentioning, though, that I once got this card every day for two weeks straight, and then my house was robbed, so please do listen to your gut about these things.)

This is a situation where you can't really be yourself and are robbed of your autonomy and self-expression. In and of itself, except when read literally, this is a pretty queer card already. Very few non-marginalized people deal with loss of autonomy or inauthentic self-expression the way that people of color, queer people, disabled folks, and marginalized women do. Even so, the specific applications to the LGBTQQIP2SA+ community in the Seven of Swords come down to microaggressions or specific hurtful situations. The Seven of Swords is your biphobic spouse, your homophobic grandmother, or a doctor who won't let you start HRT without therapy. It's an office place that donates to the Pride Festival every year but doesn't offer health insurance for domestic partners. It's the well-meaning dad who says, "Don't tell your grandma, though, this will kill her." It's all of those things that remind us of larger societal or personal traumas that compound those messages and leave us feeling boxed in without a voice of our own. This card is primarily a warning or a reminder to deal with that hurt and pain in real time, as much as you may want to suppress them. When you are being boxed in or when your voice is being silenced, you have to deal with it in the moment. The seeker is being called to fight their way out of that box and to learn to move on from there.

Sometimes in the queer community we are all so hurt and fighting so many battles that we turn that pain inside out within our own spaces and community. The Swords are also our cards of words and technology, so this is especially pertinent in online spaces. Call-out culture and infighting absolutely have their place, but that culture can also be toxic or emotionally abusive and usually hits trans people and POC the hardest. This culture can make the querent feel as if their voice doesn't matter, their trauma is irrelevant or invisible, or that their quest for more education to better themselves is in vain.

With the Five of Swords we're looking at a situation where it may be time to back out of the argument. Perhaps you really were in the wrong and it's time to stop fighting and face that reality. Alternatively, perhaps no one is in the wrong, and the situation has become too heated to reach a resolution. There's a good chance you're even in the right with the Five of Swords but fighting will not lead to a conclusion right now. It will only lead to more fighting or end up exhausting you. Take a breath, decide if this fight is a good idea, and move away from it when you inevitably decide it's time.

The Seven of Swords, however, is a little trickier. This card is less about heat and tension turned inward and more about known abusers (of any kind) and how easily they seem to move through so-called safe spaces so long as they, too, are queer. The Seven shows the harmful effect this has on the survivor, and unfortunately, to be removed from the path of that abuser, the seeker may have to leave that space, forum, or even close group of friends. This is not a happy or easy card, and so it does not offer happy or easy solutions. If your chosen family is perpetrating emotional abuse or allowing it to go unchecked, it is time to move on. If an online forum offers nothing but silencing and fighting, it may be time to head out. If the romantic relationship that once brought you so much joy when you were young and newly out of the closet now makes you feel trapped or unable to be your full, true self, it is time to end it and move forward with as much vigor as you can muster, albeit a little worse for wear.

THE SIX OF SWORDS

There is a beautiful break in the suit of Swords from the oppression and trauma of the Five and Seven, and it sits right in between the two. The Six of Swords offers hope and promise in the middle of those rougher waters. This card most often depicts someone on a boat, traveling over water to a better time. The travel is bittersweet. We may be leaving something that is hard or even tragic to walk away from. But it is a rite of passage, something we must do to move on and move forward in our lives. Though the travel itself is difficult, what lies ahead are clear waters, healing, and happier times. In time, our sadness and pain will fade and we will be rejuvenated. I have always loved the Six of Swords. I love seeing this card of logically making the best decision for ourselves and our lives being tempered with the emotional and healing water borrowed from the much happier suit of Cups. I love seeing that though this journey is the seeker's, they are not alone. I love the ambiguity of whose story this is. Is it the person steering the ship or the person calmly seated, contemplating their past and future? I also love that this card allows us to live in murkier times without trying to cut away our emotions—it just wants us to stay on track and know that this heaviness is fading.

This is a card of journeys and of change, and even when those do weigh heavier on our hearts, they are almost always for the best. When I came out of the closet I was stuck in limbo (by which I mean the notorious Bible Belt of the Southeastern United States). I was in love and it didn't work out. I had new queer friends and other chosen family, but I was still stuck in a place that was damaging to me, that liked me better when I was in the closet, and that wanted me gone as badly as I wanted to be gone. I suffered for probably three years, stuck in that Five of Swords oppression, until one day someone said to me, "Why don't you just leave?" They weren't being kind, but it was the best thing anyone has ever said to me to this day. When you are fighting mental health issues, outside oppressors, and your past, cutting through to something simple and pure is impossible.

That's what the Swords cards do for us though—they become that person that says, "Why don't you just leave?" In my case this card came to represent the journey I took to the Midwest. Leaving to finish school in a then-blue state meant leaving my closest friends, an ex-partner that I was still determined to make it work with, and the mountains that I worshipped. Yet it was right for me, and it was necessary. My road to the Midwest was littered with hiccups and regret—until I got there, and for the first time I felt like I could breathe.

That then is our first hard but true queering of the Six of Swords. Many of us feel trapped in small towns. It feels like that Five of Swords environment might actually get the best of us. In truth, some of us actually are trapped, and I don't mean to sound insensitive to that reality, and other cards do address that head-on. In many cases, though, we can just . . . leave. We can find somewhere queerer, weirder, more liberal, more radical, or more like what a home is supposed to be. If the Six of Swords is showing up and you hate where you live, think through that for a while. What's keeping you there? What would you be losing? And is it that trade-off worth it?

Another queering of the Six of Swords comes after a move, a change, or that bittersweet transition. I mentioned earlier that this card is swirling with the healing and emotions promised by the symbolism of water. As LGBTQQIP2SA+ seekers we often find ourselves at a place in our lives that is actually pretty good, yet we still don't feel right or like we think we should. The Six of Swords then calls us to go on a metaphorical healing journey so that we can appreciate where we are. I don't know any LGBTQQIP2SA+ people who don't deal with pain from our past or struggle with the trauma of living in a queerphobic society or both. There are years on end we deny our reality, and even if everyone and everything else in our life is perfect, there is likely some long-term damage.

This Six then comes to push (or row) us to something warmer, calmer, and better—but we have to be willing to take the journey first. Are we willing to cut out the things that still hurt us, be they internal or external? Are we able to dive into our own depths and revisit the pain we try to suppress so that we can truly overcome it? Those choices are ours to make, but the Six of Swords promises we will reach a better place if we do.

The Six of Swords also has some more straightforward, practical applications as we queer it, but the message is still the same. If your employer doesn't offer health care that covers your transition needs, it might be time to move on. If your chosen family has done nothing but quarrel for two years, it might be time to assess your need for them. If your relationship hurts you more than it supports you . . . well, you know. These are never easy answers, and the Six of Swords doesn't promise any. What it does do is encourage you to go on that journey anyway and promise that, over time, you'll be content with the result.

As a final note, a queer Six of Swords does show up when you are already on the journey sometimes, as in, when you are already in that boat in the middle of a body of water and not sure where you're going. Look ahead, not behind in these cases. Remember why you are moving, or healing, or venturing out on your own. Allow the sudden spike in your emotions to exist so that your queer identity and your choices as a human can be affirmed and nurtured by your healing. This card says that you're not wrong to feel sad or uncertain. Your feelings and experience are valid. Yet this journey you are on can take you so much further than you ever thought. Trust that more and better is coming—because it is. Eventually that Swords logic will cut through the confusion and the hurt will fall away as you walk toward brighter shores.

THE EIGHT, NINE, AND TEN OF SWORDS

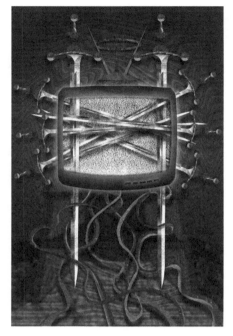

The Swords are not the kindest suit. They represent something quite dark that many of us have trouble facing: our own shadow selves. This is apparent throughout the whole suit, though we haven't really dived in yet. Yes, the Five and Seven represent oppressive forces, but they also show our own inability to cope or the idea that we do often feel trapped and small because of those situations. This is a side of ourselves that these cards push us to come to terms with. However, our shadow selves are never more present than they are in the Eight, Nine, and Ten of Swords.

The Eight of Swords is a card that often features someone seemingly bound while surrounded by swords and maybe water. Upon closer look, we see that they're not actually bound very tightly or closely at all. The card is really about feeling stuck more than being stuck. It's about an inability or unwillingness to see things as they are, more than it is about something external clouding your vision. The Nine of Swords most often features someone trapped and constrained by their own fears, and in many cases anxiety and depression are indicated here even by readers who otherwise wouldn't look for that. The Ten shows the worst-case scenario that started in the Eight coming to fruition; we are bottoming out, or we have been stabbed in the back. The Tens often represent transformation, and in the Swords (our suit of mental illness and other traumas), transforming looks like real pain from where you least expect it. Or . . . this Ten represents the way we manifest our darkest desires for self-destruction and chaos. We start feeling trapped in the Eight, and even though we know we should break away, we don't. We let the anxiety of the Nine consume us until eventually we bring that Ten into being. Our shadow selves have been formed and shaped by the pain and struggle

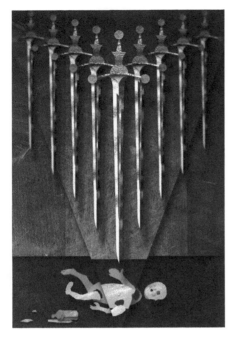

we have overcome, and they warn us of the danger in repeating the cycles that have led us astray before.

So what does that mean for us as queer people? These three cards already deal pretty heavily and significantly with mental illness and loss, but as the Swords keep reminding us, those things are often doubly true for seekers who are LGBTQQIP2SA+. What are the anxieties we are currently facing, and how does that correspond to our gender and sexual anxiety? I am personally spending way too much time feeling immobilized like the Eight by our current political situation in the United States, and it has often led me to that fearful, panic-inducing Nine of Swords. The Ten in this case affirms our fears as real, and that is a hard, harsh lesson that all marginalized people do have to learn at some point: sometimes this isn't anxiety. Sometimes it is our intuition and things really are as bad as they seem. Still, the lessons of the Eight and Nine stand. If the Ten is coming no matter what, perhaps there is a better way to deal with our collective trauma than shutting down.

I want to be crystal clear that in instances of mental illness and trauma it is very often beyond our control when our mind or body starts reacting in unhealthy ways. If these cards are coming up, though, there is likely another way to process or handle everything going on around you. The Swords are our cards of logic and left-brain thinking, and with that comes the idea of medicine, treatment, and meditation. The Eight through Ten often warn us that we need something different or more to get through the next phase, either because our illness is too strong or the attacks are too big.

In our microcosms, queer querents see these bigger patterns play out in our relationships, careers, and roles as activists, too. LGBTQQIP2SA+ relationships often come with much higher stakes, in part because there are fewer of us and we become determined to hold on even when we shouldn't, and also in part because we are

QUEERING THE TAROT

often making an active choice *not* to push our feelings down until we barely feel them anymore. Because the stakes are higher, our heartbreaks and endings of friendships often feel much more like swords to the gut than the incredibly sad but often manageable heartbreak cards from other suits. In the case of romantic or close platonic relationships, the Eight and Nine are warning you that you're reaching a breaking or tipping point. You're either not asking for help when you should be, not pulling out when all signs point to the need to do so, or collapsing in on yourself instead of facing the problems in a relationship head-on. This starts with that Eight, which so very often indicates the self-doubt that is a trademark in so many queer people.

You're not just feeling stuck in this Eight as a queer person, though; you're doubting your gut instinct and refusing to see your third eye's visions. When you spend half your life doubting that you even are who you know you are or being told that you're wrong about yourself, you can't just get over the self-doubt that plagues you afterward. You can spend time and energy building yourself back up slowly over time, but it starts with taking off this blindfold in the Eight and allowing yourself to become aware of what's really going on.

Otherwise this same pattern plays out—the Nine brings in so much stress and overwhelm that we can barely function, let alone address the problems in our relationships. This will ultimately lead to the Ten where either we are right and our friend or partner has left us, or we were wrong that it was ending but because we withdrew, it did. This same short story can be applied to jobs where we are not out of the closet and communities and activist roles we devote ourselves to. If we allow the Eight to keep us stuck, the Nine keeps us pinned and terrified, then the Ten sees the fallout out of that and leaves us scrambling to deal with cleaning up the mess.

In a lot of tarot decks, though, that background behind the anguish of the Ten of Swords doesn't look so bad. Sometimes a sun is rising slowly. Sometimes an ocean calmly laps at the shore, begging you to come closer to the healing water. In one of my most beloved decks, there is a phoenix pictured. As marginalized people we need to be warned and aware of when things are about to hit the fan. That's what many of the Swords do for us. We also need empowerment and reminders of how strong we are. This is likely not our first defeat, and it will probably not be our last. Still, as queer people we rise and start over, again, and again, and again. This is where the numbered swords leave us as LGBTQQIP2SA+ seekers—looking to that rising sun, knowing we will love and fight and win again.

4

THE SUIT OF PENTACLES

I didn't connect with Pentacles for a long time. It felt like this suit was so much about materialism in a way I didn't believe in and family in a heteronormative way that I couldn't relate too. Over time, though, this has become the most patient and reassuring set of cards in the tarot to me. My queerplatonic partner and I have carved out an incredibly unconventional home filled with unicorn masks, witchcraft, and love that no one understands—least of all us. It is still a home that is stable for our romantic partners, for the friends that come for game nights, and most importantly, for ourselves. The Pentacles started making a little more sense then, but I still struggled with the materialism I saw as inherent in them. Then my careers, which I am deeply passionate about, started taking off. It was never about the money, but wow, it feels great to succeed on my own terms. Then I fell into a wonderful group of queer friends where resource building and sharing sit at the core of our connection and love for each other. Somewhere in all of this, the Pentacles started standing above the rest of the deck when I needed comfort, love, and reassurance.

Queering the Pentacles is as easy as taking stock of what means something in your own queer life. It's as simple as thinking about what you're trying to grow and develop. It's as important as changing the world at large, though this suit primarily relates to self, family (chosen or otherwise), and community. Big change starts within, let's not forget that, though as queer or otherwise marginalized people we owe other people like us all of the fire we have inside of ourselves. Living our lives joyfully and with firm roots in the ground is also a form of resistance. This is something other LGBTQQIP2SA+ people can look at and say, "Hey, that's where I want to be: comfortable and happy." In allowing ourselves the luxury of the Pentacles we are telling other queer people that they deserve luxury. In finding homes and families that we don't see on TV but do feel deeply in our souls, we promise others that they can find that, too. Living a full life in a world that hates you *is* resistance, and that's the type of resistance that the Pentacles push us to. You've likely spent so much of your life battling personal trauma, collective trauma, and the daily trauma of living in a queerphobic world. Regardless of who is or isn't watching, you deserve a safe space to breathe, and that is what the Pentacles bring.

The Pentacles, for anyone, are all about slow growth. You've got to plant your seeds, and you've got to let them thrive on their own terms. As such, I've broken from my Minor Arcana format, giving each card its space to breathe and grow, and allowing this suit to become whatever it needs to for you.

THE ACE OF PENTACLES

We start, then, with the Ace of Pentacles. If Aces bring news or are news, the literal quick translation of this card is, "News of family, home, or career—likely positive." This is a happy and straight-shooting card. If you've been looking for your dream house, you're probably going to find it. If you've been stuck in a dead-end position in a field you love, you're probably moving ahead pretty soon. Unexpected money shows up, including inheritances because of this suit's ties to family (though it's probably not anyone unexpected or whom you are super close to). As a more spiritual card or energy, the Ace of Pentacles is a call to put down roots, to create a home, or to build or provide a resource. It's a promise that you're safe now, and safety means you're at an exciting time where you can grow or develop anything you want and know that something good will come out of it, even if you don't quite know what that something is. This card is a good omen and a great opportunity, and it's definitely assuring you that *now* is the time to put down roots.

As career or financial news, a queering doesn't change this card much but it does give it some nuance. In a world where in many states you can get fired for coming out as transgender or having a same-sex partner, career advancement is a welcome breath. Given the aforementioned disproportionate levels of poverty, finding out you're moving beyond that is amazing news. It's also healing in a way that I don't think it would be for someone who wasn't working at the intersections of poverty and another marginalized identity. That means that with a queer Ace of Pentacles we see an aspect of the card that we haven't before: healing from past trauma and moving forward confidently, even if the manifestation of that is material and worldly.

This card is pretty straightforward, even when deconstructing it or queering it, but we can use it to dig a little deeper. The Ace of Pentacles is promising that whatever you're looking for, your chosen queer family is right around the corner or it's perhaps telling you that what you need is right in front of your face. My queer-platonic partner struggled for years to find their footing in their family, until they accepted the love that I, their grandma, and so many of our dear friends offered so freely and unconditionally. This card is very much about accepting the Earthly blessings we already have, and for many people, family that has previously not understood our identity or life comes around with this Ace.

In this day and age, what so many of our queer families need are actual resources. Queer people, especially those of color, live in poverty at an incredibly disproportionately high rate. What we need is food security, friends with extra rooms, and knowing we'll have a way to get to the work or odd jobs we do find. This card could show up to tell you that those resources already exist in your area if you open yourself up to them. It could also mean that you are in a place to start providing those resources for others. If you're making a decent amount of money and have been wondering how to give back, think about what your local queer community needs and find a way to do that. If you cook well, find somewhere that will host community meals a few times a week. Find someone who knows who's homeless in your community and how to distribute armfuls of blankets and gloves to those who need them in the cold. You don't have to do everything, but this card often shows you're in a place to do something, and that is powerful knowledge that you can and should put into action quickly.

THE TWO OF PENTACLES

This card of balance and fluctuation is a necessary evil in our Earthly journey. If the Ace promises news and growth, the Two reminds us that life is still life. That brilliant business adventure will hit some snags and potentially even lose money to start. Our dream home will see a pipe burst. Our family, chosen or otherwise, will still fight because it is comprised of other human beings who each have their own trauma and emotional needs. We will start that valuable resource for our community, and then we will see it run dry at times. That's okay; yes, there's fluctuation and it's hard. It's also absolutely critical for us as we learn to grow and thrive. We do not know who we are based solely on the best of times; we know who we are when we have suffered and handled it. That is balance, taking the bad with the good and learning to find the funny story or the warm hug in the middle of it all.

A card of balance in a suit about career, money, home, and family also reminds us that there are other things in life. There's our spiritual journey, our friendships, the fact that we like sitting on our couch and binge-watching *The Gilmore Girls.* There are a million aspects of life, and this card reminds us that they all need our attention right now. I get this card a lot as a multipassionate (someone with careers and goals in multiple fields), telling me that now is not the time to slow down anywhere and I just have to handle it and keep going. Yet it also shows up to remind me that I have a sick body and a traumatized heart, and sometimes I just really need that Netflix binge. It's not contradictory at all; rather every message of this card reminds us to nurture all parts of ourselves.

As a bonafide queer person who is disabled and has struggled forever with poverty, I sometimes feel like my whole life has been about learning to navigate the Two of Pentacles. That's not at all unusual for *any* LGBTQQIP2SA+ person, but especially those who are wading through multiple intersections of marginalization. In our activist lives we see it daily. As soon as we gain a cool piece of legislation, we lose another one we were counting on. In the personal, it so very often seems like one step forward and two steps back to create a safer art space, food shelf, or youth program for our community. I have a day where I feel out and proud and great, and then a day when I feel scared and small. Some of this imbalance is important for learning. Do I still create space when a physical space is lost, and how? Do I still behave bravely on days when I don't feel strong? Sometimes, though, I have learned all of these lessons, and what I needed was another good day for queer people, and receiving something different is jarring. Unfortunately the Universe (or any Divine you believe in) and the world around us don't always behave specifically according to what I, as one person, need. Sometimes someone else needed that win more, and sometimes someone else fought harder to get their idea through. That's life, and that is also balance.

So where does the Two of Pentacles take us queer kids in those darker times? The most important keyword in this card is balance. Our whole lives we have striven to find ourselves and live our lives as those selves no matter what was going on in the world around us. That is unequivocally a lesson in balance. When you can find yourself, your voice, and your heart at the center of the whirlwind, you have found true balance. That's what the Two of Pentacles urges the marginalized to do when it shows up. This card wants you to think through what makes you feel calm, centered, and focused no matter what is falling down around you. You need that center in the worst of times, sure. You also need it in the best of times when everything is happening quickly and unapologetically. You want to retain your place in your community, your home, your body, and so you must quickly learn to find that inner peace. That is the biggest and most important lesson in the Two of Pentacles, and something every queer person needs to have tucked away in their self-care toolkit. The world will continue to be cruel and kind to us in turn, and as survivors of this floating ball in the sky, we've got to find a way to make it work.

THE THREE OF PENTACLES

The Three of Pentacles is a card where step-by-step methods of gain pay off. It's a card where collaboration is queen. It's a card where slow and steady really, really does win the race. After an Ace of sudden news and opportunity and a Two where things look a little less steady, this Three promises that the effort you put in after the Ace pays off. Working with others is also well aspected, and longtime dreams of collaboration often come to fruition. In *The Spiral Tarot,* one of my oldest and dearest decks, we see a ballerina being applauded and praised for their work. I've internalized this card, then, to also mean that the right people are paying attention, and that's what will lead to your day in the spotlight. Ballet is tedious, hard work and it's easy for dancers to feel disheartened or discouraged. Yet here one is, with every bit of that work paying off because someone saw enough in them to grant them a role where a whole room full of people would stand up and applaud. It's a beautiful card, and one I've cried upon receiving. This work might feel thankless, but your loved ones, your superiors at work, your favorite deity—they're watching, and you're going to be so thrilled that you took all the right steps to get here.

As an LGBTQQIP2SA+ person, this card also lends itself to the activist collective in spite of the microcosmic nature of the Pentacles suit. Brick by brick, we are building a better world. Little by little, the people in charge are noticing. Piece by piece, we are covering up the scars that our kyriarchy has left on its individuals. That's magickal. It's also logical. Along this line, when we're talking about resource building and giving back to our community, this card urges us not to get discouraged too easily. Maybe no one hears about your space or opportunity at first, but a Three of Pentacles tells you to stick with it. The right people will hear about it, and you will end up giving back and making your mark in your community.

Because this suit is so personal, I have seen mountains moved in clients' families of origin with this card. There are clients who get a lot of pushback on their identity from their family but who don't want to give up or disown them. No one *has* to make that choice, but it is a totally valid (and totally human) one to make. The Three of Pentacles does promise those querents that the work of trying to open those hearts and minds will pay off and better yet, assures us that we have allies in the situation even if we don't know it.

The Three of Pentacles is one that almost always shows up regarding career. It has those other manifestations I've talked about, but nine times out of ten, this is a career card. Many of us who are LGBTQQIP2SA+ have our identities built into our career or branding, or are professional policy makers and activists. This card essentially promises that those were worthwhile chances to take. We see the right clients coming to us, the right supervisors paying attention, and we see that other people's identities or allyship come to our rescue and push us from where we are to the next step. This is a card where I urge people not to hide in their careers. It's a card of assets, and trusting that the assets we use will bring about the conclusion we desire. We are our own greatest asset, though, and the Three of Pentacles promises we can put our whole queer selves in the spotlight and come out with the stability and career growth we crave.

THE FOUR OF PENTACLES

The Four of Pentacles denotes success, but it's one I've always had a hard time connecting with. The figure pictured in a traditional *Rider-Waite-Smith Tarot* deck is holding on to his coins tightly, refusing to let anyone else touch them—and refusing to take chances or move forward in his own life for fear of losing them. This, then, is a card about conservatism and, worse yet, stinginess. It's a card that leads to loneliness, and it's a card that indicates a wildly unpleasant, if technically successful, life. This Four shows up when someone is overly concerned with the financial part of a career they don't love, but the most common manifestation I see in clients and friends is more of a metaphor. If this card is about being ungenerous, that doesn't always mean money. Most people getting tarot readings are not money-centric to a fault the way that this card indicates, though it has had the traditional applications when querents were asking about their boss, a parent, or a partner where things were turning sour. Most often, though, this is a card of holding your hand too close to your chest and refusing to let go of information people close to you may need about your inner workings. It's very often a card of not being generous of heart or spirit and can indicate a seeker who wants to open their heart but can't. Much like the traditional figure holds his coins close to his body, if this card is showing up as you or an energy you're putting out there, it's showing you that you are holding your mysteries, secrets, or capacity for love too tightly and keeping them too internal.

As LGBTQQIP2SA+ people, it's a really common temptation to fall into. We get messages and coding from the society around us all the time that the way we love or even the way we are isn't right. After enough of these messages become internalized, we don't trust when love (in any form) crosses our path. We hold our hearts tightly in our own hands no matter what our queer community or a potential partner does to earn us opening up a little bit. The nature of this card running through my veins is one of my greatest weaknesses as a human. So I know, and I get it. That fear of being hurt, and not only losing someone we could have loved, but also proving this hurtful world right about us, seeps into how we treat the people who are actually worth our hearts. This card shows up mostly as a warning. "This is what you're doing. Please stop." Or sometimes more politely, "It's okay to let your guard down now."

Alternatively, this card often indicates that this is what someone else in your life is doing or going through. It may not be personal, and if anything they may be desperately trying to let you in, yet they grip themselves so tightly that you cannot find your way. This is not your fault. Unfortunately, though, it may not change. You have to decide if those pieces of themselves they are clutching are precious enough to wait for. They may be—but the reality is it may be time to walk away. You're not a friend's or partner's therapist. This is not your job. You are dealing with someone who likely has years or decades of holding too tightly under their belt, and sometimes it's better to walk away and work through your own stuff.

I don't want to overlook the elements of control in the Four of Pentacles and how they can manifest negatively in our lives. Sometimes people hold on to themselves too tightly, but sometimes they hold on to others too tightly. There are times when this is okay. You want someone in your life who is going to fight for you and your love, but this card isn't that. There are times when our cards about control become fun explorations into BDSM and kink, but this card isn't that either. This card is someone who may need to know your every move and who may need to control every facet of how the relationship is going. This card is someone who ultimately wants to control you in an overbearing, abrasive, and abusive way. Abuse is not uncommon in queer relationships, and it's unfortunately all too common for bisexual and transgender people to be abused by their partners. Furthermore, there often aren't resources to help them leave those relationships. As a community, we are even more scared than mainstream society to call out abuse. We don't want people looking at our relationships as bad or our identity as reason for abuse. So we keep quiet, and we don't call out. That is, to put it mildly, a mistake. I digress a bit—other cards will let us know when it's time to take a stand publicly. The Four of Pentacles' job is to urge us to leave that partner, friend, or family member. Immediately.

The Four of Pentacles is a card that I've seen straight, cisgender readers read positively. In a spiritual community, this has always confused me. Materialism is, generally speaking, not good. I'm not someone who doesn't value my work, and I absolutely see spiritual work as real work. Yet if we're hustling for the money to the point that we lose our hearts, what's the point? Why take a spiritual path at all? I love money—but it's not why I do what I do. As an LGBTQQIP2SA+ person, I've tried to put a spin on it regarding resource building and sharing, but it still comes up negative. Specifically, it comes up as someone who has the resources to lift our community up but won't share or contribute. Remember why we're even queering the tarot, though. As marginalized people, our point of view is going to be much different from someone else's. (Plus my whole thesis as a tarot reader is that every card is different to every person.) If you can't turn the wealth yet stinginess, the success yet coldness of the Four of Pentacles into something good, don't. Question the things we place on pedestals as a society, and know that for every strictly negative card in the deck, there are seven more cards ready to promise you healing and adventure.

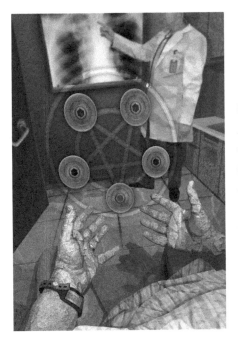

THE FIVE OF PENTACLES

I promise the Pentacles get cheerful again! Just not right now. Fives in general are our cards of duress and heartbreak, and this one specifically speaks to financial loss and poverty. Pentacles are Earth energy, and Earth is anything that keeps us connected to the world around us and allows us to grow and thrive. That means this Five also speaks to feeling isolated and disconnected, and it can include feeling lost or alone spiritually (or existentially). This is a hard card and one where it's easy to get down on yourself and lost in your emotions. I don't want to overlook a very common piece of the artwork in this card, though; often the card shows a couple of people lost or stuck in the snow while they look in on a lush room filled with happy people. There are two ways to interpret that. One is that, yeah, wow, this really is a hard time you're going through, and you're 100 percent right to feel like it isn't fair or justified. It can also be taken as a warning not to compare yourself and your life to others. In the heyday of the Internet and Instagram and all of our wonderful apps, it's easy to look at what other people seem to have (and are boasting about) and feel low about where we are and how we're doing. Depending on how you see this card, there are two different outlets for those feelings. You can use that stable Earth energy to figure out how to move forward yourself, or you can just . . . stop. Stop comparing yourself to other people, because where you are now is where you are. If you can change it, this card is a necessary message to do so. If you can't, you're only going to hurt yourself more by staring in vain at what other people have.

In my own life, this card has shown up when I get the blues about not being romantically partnered, or when it feels like my life is behind schedule because a lot of my college friends are two or more kids in already. Sometimes the card shows up because it wants me to recognize where maybe I am a little behind schedule, but more often than not it is that stark reminder to stop comparing myself to my (often straight and cisgender) age peers. I don't want a family in the traditional way, and that's a pretty common (though certainly not unilateral) mind-set in the LGBTQQIP2SA+ community. It's ridiculous then that the feelings of inadequacy and "What am I even doing with my life?" creep in when I see that Betsy from Advanced Geometry is on her third kid, but it happens with stark regularity.

As we queer this card, we need to look at the realities of life for a queer seeker, and while not having a partner is not life threatening, it does lead into that feeling of isolation and certainly makes us feel lost at times. The reality is that it's harder to date in the queer community, especially when you're over thirty. That's fine! Everyone who is single needs the occasional reminder to stop comparing yourself to other people and their relationships. In a community that makes up less than 5 percent of the population, the odds are a little stacked against you. Be gentle on yourself.

Of course I'm not going to ignore the effects of poverty on querents from the LGBTQQIP2SA+ community and how this card plays a hand. Another one of those realities I mentioned above is something I've brought up several times already in this book: housing, employment, and stability very often do not come easily or securely to us. In a card of poverty or financial loss, we do need to take that into account. Unfortunately, we are likely still climbing uphill the best we can when this card shows up. Nonprofits and community resources fold, and this Five isn't going to lie to us if a resource we are building is heading that way. Our personal financial lives can be in shambles for the foreseeable future because of how poverty intersects with other marginalized identities. It can all be a tough pill to swallow. That can also be valuable information. It could be that we needed to hear our current path wasn't about to lead to success so we can switch gears. It could be the final straw that encourages us to seek help and resources. It could be that sometimes we need to struggle before we move ahead in our journey, which the Pentacles do promise in the following cards.

Another harsh reality for queer seekers is the spiritual poverty often seen in this card. So many of us grew up Christian, Muslim, or Jewish in churches, mosques, and temples that didn't want us once we came out. The temptation to turn away from our gods or spirituality on the whole is nearly impossible to resist when we are pushed away from religious communities that once felt like home. It's an unpopular opinion, I know, but I actually think that time of feeling separated from your Higher

Power is good. Religion should be deeply personal, and until you are metaphorically lost in the dark woods, you are never going to find your personal sunrise. Some LGBTQQIP2SA+ people are very Christian, very Muslim, very Jewish, and many of them find a spiritual home that lets them be both; still I think this is something you have to find for yourself. This card is not a fun one, but a time to question is an opportunity, and it's an opportunity that leads many of us to a deep, primal understanding of ourselves and our spirits if we let ourselves lose our way for a while.

THE SIX OF PENTACLES

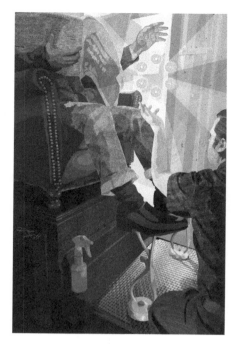

The Six of Pentacles traditionally features a successful, prosperous figure handing out money to those less fortunate than themselves. As readers, we learn that this means it's either time to give to back, or time to accept help, depending on your own situation or the surrounding cards. If you are seeing more money than usual, this card is encouraging you to use some of that money to help others, pay back old debts, give to charity, or make investments that improve your community. If you identify more with the beggars on the card than the wealthy person, this card is telling you to suck up your pride and ask for help. There are people and organizations that would be thrilled to help you get back on your feet—all you need to do is ask. This can, of course, be a metaphor. Generosity of spirit, heart, and knowledge are all highly valuable, and often necessary for forging new friendships or keeping our family lives healthy. When this card comes up, it's time to open yourself up, or accept that a loved one is truly being generous and kind with themselves right now.

This card fits in beautifully with conversations about building community resources and making sure that, as a queer community, we are all provided for. Either you have exactly what is needed to provide a resource, amplify voices, or protect people in your community—or you're in need, and need to trust that the underground infrastructure that your queer friends are running and contributing to can and will support you. One thing I know that many LGBTQQIP2SA+ people deal with is the question of what to do when we're out of poverty. We aren't always going to be happy making investments that pay off only for ourselves, but buying up property we can rent affordably or run a food shelf from will make us feel truly successful and capable.

For queer seekers, the emotional aspects of this card are especially relevant. I have certainly seen it mean, "It's time to get help" or, "It's time to give back," but what I usually see when the Six of Pentacles shows up is LGBTQQIP2SA+ querents who have come out of traumatic situations and backgrounds and who have trouble trusting those around them. If your parents kicked you out because they found out you were a sexual or gender minority, if they were abusive, or if they were great parents until they learned your truth, you're going to have a lot of trouble getting and finding your bearings as you try to form adult relationships. This is also true if you were in an abusive relationship, had a dangerously toxic friendship, or even just spent years feeling stuck in solitude because no one around you understood you. There are many cards that speak to this trauma though; what the Six of Pentacles wants you to know is that the people in your daily life now, the ones offering you a shoulder to cry on, a fun game night, or a warm meal, are people you can trust and it is safe to let your guard down around them.

This card comes up a lot for me now as the person being called on to share of themselves. I spent so long overcoming my own trauma and learning to share my opinions without my voice shaking that I didn't realize I had somehow evolved past just surviving; I became, without realizing it, someone with a story to share and a heart ready to love openly, without the conditions I was so used to putting on my love. Healing is not a perfect arc, and it's not every day I'm sitting in that position. It is certainly more frequent as I continue on my journey, and it is certainly nowhere I ever expected to be. The Six of Pentacles is not only a calling to love more and be generous, but also an assurance that it is safe to do so. It's a card that shows how much you've grown and how much you've moved past in your life, and it's a card that encourages you to let others see all of the sides of you that got you here.

THE SEVEN OF PENTACLES

The Seven of Pentacles is a card I learned a little bit differently from most people and a card that is radically different whether you're studying a *Thoth*-based deck or a *Rider-Waite-Smith*–based deck. The things they all have in common is that the Seven starts the metaphor that we see through the end of this suit about planting season. In a *Thoth*-based deck, this is a card about a ruined harvest. In a *Rider-Waite-Smith*–based deck, it's a card about how you've already done a substantial part of your work. You've planted your seeds, and now it's time to take a step back and let them grow on their own. I was learning tarot at a harrowing time in my life, though. The whole world was new and a bit terrifying, but I knew it was time for me to plant my own seeds and make my own way. The art in the tarot allows for all three of these interpretations, but your deck should make it pretty clear which way it leans. Regardless, this card kick-starts a time of hard work and innovation for the seeker and also encourages us to take things one step at a time, allowing space for natural growth cycles.

For LGBTQQIP2SA+ people, the Seven of Pentacles can be an exciting but also terrifying time. Whoever we have been and whoever we are now, it is time to contemplate our next steps. Whether we have seen an attempt at a new life get overturned and ruined, have done the planting and are waiting to see what happens, or it is time to start the planting, the Seven of Pentacles will show up to let us know that this is our time and our field to create in. The trade-off, though, is that it's time to start thinking about the big picture and where we want to be in fifteen years. We all have goals for the next week, month, or year, but the Seven of Pentacles wants us to go a step further and actually focus on the things we hope to accomplish by the end of our lives, but likely haven't started yet.

Why specifically do I bring up queer people here? Because often it isn't until later in life, or at least after several journeys of self-discovery, that we can even begin to start on those higher goals. We spend the first part of our lives questioning our intuition, our ability to love, our attractions to other people, and our very identities. Then comes all of the analyzing and unpacking and processing. Next comes, most often, a weird period of time where we *could* move on, but we understandably like sitting where we are and just enjoying being queer and happy and healthy. And after all of that comes the Seven of Pentacles. It's a much different trajectory from our classmates and siblings who are both straight and cisgender, and it means that the Seven of Pentacles is often a surprise for us. We don't see that day sneaking up where we're ready to take control and plant the seeds we've been carrying with us, but it's here, and the card shows up asking what we're going to do now.

That doesn't mean everything is easy. Taking control of your own life and regaining your autonomy means that you are now responsible for the ups and downs. If that Seven does come as ruin, you and you alone are responsible for righting that. From a queer perspective, though, even that is thrilling. This is your time to shine, and your time to create a harvest from a pile of weeds. If ever there was a queer skill set, the ability to turn that mess into something beautiful and sustenant would be it. This is what the marginalized spend their whole lives doing—looking at the pile of crap they've been handed and scrapping together a worthwhile life. This is all the Seven of Pentacles is asking you to do, and sure, it's exhausting being the one to do it all the time, but this time it's for you and your life. That's it. Sure that's more responsibility and more on you, but there are other cards that promise freedom. This card promises that if you pick up your hoe and get to work, the eventual harvest will be more than worth it, and since we're looking at queer values, this isn't just about payoff for you. The road you are paving for queer kids who come after you is crucial, and you are more than capable of doing that just by finding your own path to what you need.

THE EIGHT OF PENTACLES

It makes sense that the Eight of Pentacles, a card of literal or metaphorical apprenticeship or scholarship, follows the Seven of Pentacles. If the Seven is where we are called to plant our own seeds or right our life's wrongs, then the Eight is where we learn how to do that. This is where we find our own groove and become comfortable doing the work of running our own life. No one expects you to be a master gardener overnight, but they do expect you to do the work of the Eight of Pentacles: the work of learning, studying, and trying. This card is fun when it shows up in readings, because I've seen it be this deeper, all-encompassing message . . . and I've also seen it mean it was time to take up a new career by studying under someone or going back to school.

In the mundane, LGBTQQIP2SA+ seekers are probably thinking about going back to college or a vocational program for nonprofit work or community building, and this card is showing up as a good omen for that course. It could show up for someone who wants to learn how to do necessary work in their community but who needs a mentor or advisor first. Many queer seekers go into their schooling or adult life not sure who they are and not sure what life truly holds for them. The Eight is definitively a next-step card, but can often lead us to a calling we didn't know we had. It's important to spend some time navigating the waters after you first come out, working to simply find your footing. Once we've done that for a while, our place in our community often becomes crystal clear. That's when this Eight shows up to encourage us to gather the tools we need to build the resource or skill set our queer community needs from us.

In terms of learning and teaching, this card can also indicate taking a kink path—particularly where BDSM is concerned. It's not responsible nor realistic to assume you can wake up and just *be* a dom(me) or a sub. Most who commit to that spend some time getting to know the community as well as reading books about sex education and healthy expressions of kink. The same is true for those breaking into polyamory for the first time. This you *could* potentially pick up and just do, but it takes a while to learn *how* you are polyam. Do you want a primary partner? Do you believe in closing off your relationships at all? Do you know what your cap for how many people you can date or sleep with at once is? Even if you know in your soul that you are a polyamorous person, you probably can't answer these questions without spending some time learning and figuring it out. Some people need time just to fully understand what they like and don't like sexually as a trans person or person who enjoys sex with the same gender or sex. Bodies are weird, regardless, and those of us who are queer are more likely to take our time getting to know ours. That's a good thing, and this Eight of Pentacles shows up to let us know we can take our time and will end up much happier and more satisfied for it.

Outside of the bedroom, there is also a lot to learn about queer community—where to go, where to eat, where to see shows. The number of things to learn grows exponentially when you look into activism and community building, which we talked about earlier on. Certainly queer people are not obligated to become activists or community builders. It is more common than not if you hang around long enough, though, especially in smaller cities where there is no community to find, and so it must be built. The Eight of Pentacles encourages you to find your way in time, or perhaps bring in an unofficial mentor. Chosen family in queer community traditionally shows up when young LGBTQQIP2SA+ kids are looking for someone who can show them the ropes of being out. We see it in the formation of families in ball culture, for example, but it's something we all look for and create at some point.

The biggest way this card does manifest in our queer lives is when we are learning to pave our own way. All of the hard lessons of the Seven and needing to pull ourselves up and create something out of nothing begin to resolve in this Eight, though not as effortlessly as we would like. It is a hard, gradual learning process, but in the end we move ahead to the next card. First, though, we land here, in a place of apprenticeship, and the question to ask ourselves is not what we want to learn, but who we want to be after we learn it. That is where the real growth happens, and what the Eight has been trying to dig into all along.

THE NINE OF PENTACLES

A card of luxury, the Nine of Pentacles shows us rising to a prosperous state and offers us a chance to look around, smell the roses, and be grateful. This is one of my favorite cards in the deck, as I always need a reminder that "Hey, things are pretty good. Maybe be glad about it." This Nine of Pentacles, like all of our cards of joy in the tarot, is hard won. We planted the seeds in the Seven, we learned how to weed and nourish them in the Eight, and now everything is blooming beautifully. Our job now is to sit back and enjoy the foliage.

"Sit back and enjoy the foliage" is a message a lot of my queer clients struggle with most. For some reason, marginalized people have no problem being told that their road ahead is long and full of strife. They have no problem being told that it's time to go deep into their trauma to recover from it. I get little pushback from asking those seekers to do more work or dig deeper. Yet when I say, "Hey, look how much work you've done! Great job! Now, rest," I get, at best, blank faces staring back at me. At worst, I end up trying to convince the client that time off is good and that they deserve comfort. I get it. I struggle with this too. There is always something that needs doing in my career, in this community project I'm a part of, for my friends, for that queer kid who found my theatre company and wants help getting started in their career. At any given moment, I can list ten things that need to be done in each of these areas with little thought or prompting. I know that most of you reading this can relate. When we talked about the Ten of Wands we talked about activist burnout, and ignoring this card is one of the reasons we get there. We all work very, very hard in the queer community—all of us. Which means we all deserve time to recognize when that work is paying off, which means we all need to admire what we've built sometimes. You started with nothing. That was the lesson of the Seven. Now, here you are, two short cards later, with a thriving end result. You did this. That's beautiful. You are beautiful.

THE TEN OF PENTACLES

Tens are cards of transformation, and wow, do we earn it with Pentacles. We saw ourselves go from the Seven (or the One, depending on how you're recounting this narrative), and we built something solid, strong, and beautiful for ourselves and our loved ones. Traditionally, this Ten is a card of family legacies and inheritances. It has a masculine energy I've often struggled with. In a standard deck or reading, we're looking at a patriarch facing his end of days and deciding who will receive all of his money or land after he's gone. Obviously this doesn't resonate with me, though it is a beautiful message for the many businesspeople who see me about changes to their career or additions to their family. We see grandchildren in this card, and an extremely comfortable amount of material success. It's a good card, but it's one whose values I don't necessarily share.

When queering this card though, we go back through everything we've talked about: community, chosen family, and a life we built out of weeds and rubble. *That* is a beautiful story. That is transformation in its truest sense, and when this card comes up for queer movers and shakers, it promises that everything they're trying to build—whatever it is—will thrive long after they're gone. One thing the weirdo teen goth wannabe in me has always loved about this card is its comfortable and easy relationship with death. We may be nearing the end of a cycle here, and that may even be a physical life cycle, and yet we are promised joy, love, and that those who carry our name will carry out our legacy when we're gone. In the queer community that may not be kids or grandkids (It may be! Many queer people have otherwise traditional families and that's beautiful and wonderful too!), but it may be people whom we are in community with, whom we create art projects and build shelters with, whom we claim as family because of how we feel in our hearts and let that love thrive there.

An example of this card in action is the United States' current nationwide policy allowing for marriage equality. In the '80s in New York and all across the states, the AIDS epidemic wiped out entire generations due to homophobia, miseducation, and the way those things manifested in inadequate medical care. To add insult to very deep injury, many gay men were told their partners could not see them in the hospital as they lay dying because they weren't married. They weren't allowed to be married, but that didn't matter to those barring them from entry. Decades later, after the fight the surviving spouses and victims of AIDS started in earnest in the '80s, marriage equality was finally passed in the United States. These losses to our community and the lack of elders in major cities was, and is, a devastating blow to who we are as queer people. Yet their legacy lives on every time an LGBTQQIP2SA+ couple says, "I do." Furthermore, this is legislation that has paved the way for the fights we're seeing now. Because most of the United States sees these relationships as legally equitable, they are starting to see queer people as equitable. People are fighting en masse against transphobic bathroom bills and starting to realize the depth of the hurt from laws allowing LGBTQQIP2SA+ people to be fired or evicted simply for being themselves. This is the legacy those who fought in Stonewall left us with, and it's the legacy those who died of AIDS during that epidemic left us with. It was despicable the way we were treated—but those affected used their voice to ensure we wouldn't have to keep going through the same fights and indignities.

In the personal, it's crucial to remember that existing as a queer person is resistance in and of itself. The Pentacles remind us how much work goes into that seemingly basic act of resistance. We not only have to survive as queer people, but also to survive capitalism and all of the other oppressing factors that are not kind to marginalized people. Those of us who are POC or disabled still have to pick up our gardening shears and get to work in the Seven. The Ten promises us though that through taking the rest of the suit's advice, we do reach a point where the bare living in our lives is enough. It's enough resistance to inspire someone, it's enough perseverance to thrive, and it's more than enough to leave to your community when you go.

5

THE SUIT OF CUPS

We are ending our *Queering the Tarot* journey on my absolute favorite suit. I am a Pisces with a Pisces Moon and a Cancer rising, so this watery, emotional suit full of love, heartache, and, ultimately, complete emotional fulfillment serves as the basis of everything I do in my life. A lot of tarot readers pen this suit into being about romantic love and relationships, and there's definitely support for that in the suit itself. This suit is Water energy, and that does bring romance into our house. That means romantic and sexual love, but it also means close friendship and family ties that we benefit from and adore having. Water and emotions are about so much more, though. This is a suit that inspires and pushes us toward emotional healing. The Cups want us to be truly open with our hearts, but for most of us, that means recovering from all of the curveballs life has thrown at us. This is also a suit that pushes us to find whatever it is that's going to make us feel emotionally fulfilled. It's not just lovers and fiancés that pull Cups cards—it's career artists, those who love to travel, and anyone seeking pieces of their soul.

As we queer this suit, some of it will be fairly straightforward. We'll look at nontraditional family structures, including polyamorous families. We'll look at queer love and all of the beauty that can bring. We'll also look at how our healing processes may differ or be stalled compared to our straight and cisgender friends' and families'. The Cups speak beautifully to the fluidity many people experience in their sexual and gender identities, promising that all sides and phases of us can be loved and feel complete. This section may read more like a love song to the suit itself than a tarot book; I love Cups, and Cups love us.

THE ACE, TWO, AND THREE OF CUPS

Our first mini-narrative of the Cups suit is right at the beginning. The Ace brings news. That can mean opportunity for new love, news from a loved one, or insight that leads us to a period of emotional healing. While this Ace usually bears joyful news like a new crush returning our feelings, it can occasionally bear hard news or critical looks at ourselves that usher in that time of reflection and healing. I needed to be bailed out of a situation financially a couple of years ago. Someone important to me stepped up, and we began working toward healing a lifetime of misunderstandings and complicated emotions. That unexpected financial trouble, while real, ended up being exactly the Ace of Cups we needed. Where that takes us to is the Two of Cups.

Twos are about balance and duality, and that is especially clear in the Cups. This card is often used to indicate a relationship that *is* right; it's balanced, it's romantic, and this person likely could be your other half. Beyond that though, this signals finding balance while recovering from emotional trauma or burnout. Here we see you've bounced back and are falling in love with life all over again. This likely means you've found your emotional center even if it feels like everything is falling apart. Then there's the Three of Cups. This beauty shows a time of celebration, joy, and triumph. This traditionally means marriages, promotions, and babies, but as we look deeper we also see taking pride in our emotional growth. We see that you've gone from the quiet balance of the Two to the greater happiness and joy of the Three that allows you to socialize and celebrate as if you were never hurt at all. This quick narrative is absolutely lovely whether we're talking about bouncing back from a breakup, finding happiness for the first time, or starting new relationships or ventures.

Queering these first few Cups doesn't diminish the sense of joy and triumph they bring. If anything, it increases them. So far in *Queering the Tarot* we've talked *a lot* about how much LGBTQQIP2SA+ people often have to overcome before they can start trusting themselves and their intuition. That's true of our hearts too, and Cups definitely want us to listen to our hearts. In the Ace of Cups, we see a piece of news, insight, or an opportunity that allows queer people to follow their desire and forge a path ahead based purely on what they want. That's powerful. It's even more powerful when we see it pay off in this Two and Three. First we see that following our queer little hearts to their bliss leads us to a delightful, joyful place of balance where we are content and able to focus on what we want. I know many LGBTQQIP2SA+ people who fell into the gap of trying to please parents, teachers, or classmates. They were either trying to hide or to make up for their queerness. Their own heart's desires got lost then, until that Ace showed up. The Two brings those two halves of us together: the half that seeks approval, and the half that needs to go after what *we* want. We really can have both of those things. We just need to believe it. That takes us to the Three of Cups, which heralds a time of celebration. Celebration can certainly mean a party, a girl's night, or a happy hour with friends. It can also mean taking a deep breath, looking at your life and all of the happiness that Ace brought you, and being content.

The theme of family runs rampant through the suit of Cups. The arc of the Ace

through the Three of Cups mirrors the roller coaster those queer seekers without a supportive given family go through when they find friends, partners, or other forms of chosen family. The Ace brings those people into our lives. What we find after nurturing those relationships (and moving on to the Two of Cups) is sometimes new and astounding for us though—the love and spirit we have been giving to these people is reciprocated fully. We are and feel safe, supported, and loved. For some of us, this will be the first time we've experienced that. This card is so wonderful for those seekers who don't have the support of their given family, or who were shunned by classmates for being different. It's also important for those of us who form intense bonds over shared queerness. Even if your given family and classmates have been great, finding someone or several someones who went through the same experiences you did is life changing. It is these life-changing friendships or romantic partnerships that the Two promises.

What to do with that, then? *Celebrate it!* If you're getting the Three of Cups in a lot of your readings now that you've fallen in with a really great group of close friends or family, this card is very likely calling you to organize a get-together just to say, "Thanks," or, "Yay, us," or, "Hey, happy Tuesday! Love you!" Of course, celebrating doesn't always mean going wild. It could even be calling or sending thank-you cards to the people who have been supporting you emotionally, or just lighting a candle and thanking the Universe for bringing those people into your lives. The important thing is recognizing that your heart is safe now, wherever you are keeping it, and whomever you are keeping it with.

THE FOUR OF CUPS

Of course, coming off of the Three of Cups we *want* things to be beautiful and picturesque and perfect forever. Life is still life though, and that's why the Four of Cups comes next. This card shows up because even when we are living bold, powerful lives, our mood still swings downward. In this card, we seem to have everything we want, and yet we remain apathetic and disconnected. This card shows up a lot for people who struggle with depression or who are overcoming trauma. It's a common hope that if we just get our lives together, if we stock our days with the right people, the right jobs, the right habits, everything will be perfect from then on. So it's shocking when we do the work, hit a bunch of successes and then feel . . . nothing, at best. In my years (and years) of experience, I've seen this come up for people who took paths that weren't honoring their own wishes. They went to the college their dad went to and started working at the family business, or they married someone they thought they loved and built a life that was never meant to be theirs. Things happen. Beating yourself up about making those decisions is not your best decision right now and will only stoke the beige flames of ennui even more.

The Four instead suggests seeking connection, taking time for meditation, and reflecting on what led you to this point. Where should you have listened to your heart instead of your brain or another person? What can you do differently now? What will that mean for the rest of your life? Your mood, for whatever reason, isn't going to improve by sheer will. Time, consideration, and changes are needed if you want to find the piece that, right now, in this moment of the Four of Cups, feels like it's missing.

When we went through the Suit of Swords, we talked about the disproportion-ate levels of depression that LGBTQQIP2SA+ people live with, and certainly the real-ity of life is that countless people struggle with various forms of clinical depression. We're looking at a time in our lives when things are seemingly going right, but we are still struggling to feel connected. Depression and disassociation often come up with the Four, and that's even more true for queer seekers. Queer seekers also often live within a society that puts shame and judgment on our very existences, or makes us invisible altogether. Even with no mental illness at play, those external messages can push us into feeling unengaged with the world around us, or make us feel numb even when things are going well. We often can't and don't relate to mainstream television shows, movies, or even books. That's a lack of connection that has nothing to do with our mental state, and one that can slip into our subconscious and make us feel isolated without any hint to our conscious minds that it's happening.

Because queer seekers often feel isolated due to lack of representation in the art and media that drive much of our society, or because no one around them under-stands the struggle and confusion that purely being themselves has wrought, the fix is pretty straightforward. This card urges LGBTQQIP2SA+ querents to seek out queer media or branch out and find community where they are. Even in small towns, you usually aren't alone even when it feels like it. Look for ads for social groups, or get online and look for meet ups. I've even used dating apps and websites to find friends in my area (and that actually usually turns out much better than using them strictly for dating purposes).

Romantic loneliness shows up in this Four, too. This is a suit about interpersonal connections that does often promise romance. Even if we don't prioritize that area of our lives though, loneliness still sneaks up on us sometimes. Loneliness can cause a lot of sadness and heaviness that we associate with depression or pure ennui. If you're alone because of lack of options, it might be time to open yourself up to queer people in other cities, or find new community where you are. If you're not in a small town, it may be time to make some scary leaps. That means actu-ally getting back out there and seeing what's in store, or being willing to put your heart on the line when do you meet another LGBTQQIP2SA+ person that you click with. I would absolutely advise you to be safe if you know that there is a lot of hostility toward queer people in your area. Letting your guard down does not mean behaving carelessly or refusing to listen to your gut. Make sure you are talking to someone who is LGBTQQIP2SA+ themselves or you're in a safer space. Once you are, though, this is a time to drop your guard. Your long-term emotional health is far more important than the (slight) risk of a brutal rejection.

THE FIVE THROUGH SEVEN OF CUPS

This might seem like an odd grouping of cards to write as one, but the way these three play together has always felt very intertwined to me. We have the Five of Cups, a card of heartache and despair that follows the Four. Often this card comes because we didn't take the advice of the Four, and now we are feeling totally alone and we are devastated about it. Other times, we think we're living large in this Three of Cups joy, and now, all of a sudden we come crashing back to Earth with no warning. Still other times, we are somewhere else entirely. We are trying to follow our heart's desire and we get burned—badly. It's a card that sees us eating large amounts of ice cream in bed while our cats stare at our crying faces, bewildered. This card can be what leads to the Six of Cups, a card of nostalgia that can help or hinder us. Childhood memories often resurface, which means the sadness of the Five can leave us looking backward for answers. How could we have let this happen? Where did it all go wrong?

We can get stuck in the Six, craving reunion (or giving in to very bad ideas like meeting up with old exes), or we can progress to the Seven. This is a card where we are overwhelmed and bombarded with choices. This is made more complicated when we consider the Cups' drive to live in states of illusion and indulge in fantasies. How many of these choices are even real? How many choices are we creating with our mind, when, in reality, they were never possible to begin with? Ultimately this is a card where too many choices can be deafening—real or not. It's easy to say, "Let the dust settle," when you're not the one staring down an uncertain future. Ultimately, this card is a waiting game. Our heart may not know what's real or not, and certainly if we let ourselves live in the nostalgia and craving of the past that marks the Six, it will create options it shouldn't as we approach the Seven. Our intuition knows what's real, though, and so does our logical mind. Our friends, our families, our deities; they all know what's real too. The Seven is a time to listen to other people and other parts of ourselves to figure out how to recover from that Five, move on from that Six, and make the right decisions now.

Queer people nurture unhealthy relationships at about the same rate as the rest of the population, and that's so much of what we see in the Five through Seven of Cups; unhealthy relationships with lovers, friends, or employers creating additional problems in our lives and toying with our emotional health. It's important to note the special and specific reasons LGBTQQ-IP2SA+ querents might cling to unhealthy things or people compared to the rest of the population. For starters, if it's romantic relationships we are looking at, that scarcity mind-set is real. We are arguably less than 5 percent of the population, and depending on what gender you are and what gender or genders you are looking for, it's likely to be an even smaller percentage therein. So yes, we sometimes hold tightly to relationships that are unhealthy or even totally over, terrified that we're now destined to die alone. If it's an unhealthy employment situation showing up in any of these cards, please consider how often queer people live in poverty before advising a client (or yourself) to simply cut through the clouds and

move on. It isn't always that easy or even possible for marginalized people. Apply this message across the board to friendships, housing, and so on.

That also means even after a heartbreak in the Five that we should have learned from, fantasizing about the past in the Six and realizing it's better to move on in the Seven, those choices aren't real in a different way than other people might see them. Choices where your morals, identity, and or allyship to other marginalized groups are put on the line so that you can have basic things like a decent apartment or job that pays well are not real choices. This is the effect of a society built for a wealthy few on the backs of so many others. We have to do what we have to do, which means staring at a Seven of Cups, knowing these choices are just an illusion of choice, and deciding what is best for us in that moment. It's exhausting to even think about all of the times I was faced with an insurmountable number of options, especially when I knew that some of them were really not, or should not be, options at all.

At the last day job I ever had, I worked in the box office at a well-known theatre company. That company's season was released, and it was incredibly exclusionary to POC and women. Keeping quiet about the erasure my POC friends felt in that theatre company's season was never a real option for me. So I spoke out (publicly, a couple of times) and ended up being watched like a hawk by managers. That left me with a plethora of emotions, obstacles, and choices, none of which were real. I could stay and fight for change, which probably wouldn't work. I could leave and be strapped for cash but making great art elsewhere. I could stay, keep my head low during the workday, and ignore the stares and whispers. None of those were fair to me or to the POC members of my arts community. Eventually my heart healed from the Five of Cups. In my case this was the hurt and pain I felt knowing that it wasn't actually safe to speak out at this organization. Then came the Six, a dreamy period where I wished I hadn't left the job prior to this one, which was super queer friendly and had a POC-oriented mission, but where I really wasn't making ends meet. Finally, here I was at the Seven, looking at all of the choices I could make, and realizing that almost every single Cup was filled with half-truths and more heartbreak.

I am a reader who is always tempted to spin the cards into something positive, and there is artistic evidence for that in this run of cards. Sometimes having a lot of choices is incredibly freeing. Sometimes nostalgia and memories are fun and wonderful and warm. In the Five, most often, three cups are knocked over but two are still standing. "Look at the things that *are* working out," I've told countless clients. All of these things are true. Sometimes, though, when we're looking at the tarot as a whole, especially from a queer or otherwise marginalized perspective, things are just going to be crappy for a while. It is your job as a person to dig deep and find the positive emotions and safe heart space in spite of that. It is your job to look at that Seven of Cups and find a cup where you get to live your truth and live in love, even if there isn't one yet. It's not fair. That's a lot of extra work for us. It *is* work that will ultimately lead to fulfillment, though, and sometimes that's the best we can hope for.

THE EIGHT OF CUPS

Luckily the Eight of Cups turns things around for us pretty quickly. This card denotes a bittersweet ending. You loved this relationship, town, or job, but they're over now. That's really sad. However, the promise of this card is that you are moving on beautifully to bigger, brighter things. This is a decision that isn't made lightly. There are a lot of pieces of your heart still swimming around that last phase of your life. There probably always will be, but the time has come to make the hard decision and move on. This is one my least favorite cards in the deck to receive personally. I actually really love Death and The Tower. I can end things I do not want to look back on like nobody's business. I can burn down a truly toxic, crappy situation with the best of them. I can throw Swords at problems and just end them like it's going out of style. Yet when my own heart is on the line and I know I will always partially regret this decision, I struggle. I am likely to stay for way too long, causing more heartache than necessary when I inevitably do make the right decision. I try to find ways around making this decision until I just can't anymore.

Much of that is because of my own queerness. I have been so deeply, unbelievably hurt by so many people in various stages of my life. There was the friendship I ended because she kept going after women I was dating or interested in. There was the friend I fell for who cut me out of her life with no warning for reasons I still don't understand. There was the person who was like a parent to me who said they shouldn't even show lesbians holding hands on TV. That's just for starters. The last thing on Earth I want to do, ever, is cause anyone any fraction of the pain I've been through. Yet when my ex had clearly fallen under the throes of alcoholism, I knew she wouldn't get help if I didn't leave. When a different ex wanted me back but I had realized our relationship was really unhealthy, I had to decline in spite of my feelings for her. Those latter two examples are classic Eight of Cups decisions, especially for LGBTQQIP2SA+ people who are struggling to find their own truth as it is.

Not every Eight of Cups moment is completely selfless, though, especially not for queer seekers. I fell in love for the first time in a tiny town run by the Baptist college I attended. I had never planned to stay in the Bible Belt, and I had enough trauma in those years to make me run screaming to the Midwest with no plans on looking back. I did, however, lose the girl in making that decision. It took me literal years to get over her, knowing that had I not had big city dreams and had she not been totally enamored with small town life in spite of it all, things could have been different. I also moved away from the very small town in Iowa where I finished college as an Eight of Cups maneuver. I was totally smitten with this quiet, artsy, invisible life I had maintained as I finished school and probably could have maintained a little bit longer. But that would have meant living in Iowa with a theatre degree and a shelf full of tarot cards. I doubt I could have supported myself, and besides, I had fantasized about actual real cities since I was like, ten. I now had my college degree, and it was stupid to not head somewhere larger. So I did, and moving to Minneapolis is probably the second best decision I've ever made in my life. At the time though, it broke my heart, even though I knew it was right.

In other situations, queer people find that these Eight of Cups decisions are rooted in not wanting to trigger anyone else's trauma response, abandonment issues, or mental health but knowing that our own are at stake. Your number one job as a marginalized or traumatized person is to take care of yourself. Which means if you are in sobriety or are overcoming codependent tendencies and your partner is still struggling, you might have to bow out. If your partner is, in your mind, a really good, wonderful person but is having a hard time respecting new names and pronouns as you transition genders, it is probably not the relationship for you. If your entire group of friends once held you up and made you feel great but has gotten mean and catty lately, maybe it's time to move on. I bring up these examples because they are ones I've seen with clients over and over again. Ultimately what the Eight of Cups does is remind us that as LGBTQQIP2SA+ people we have overcome being assumed straight and cisgender in our upbringing, learned to listen to our inner voice, and somehow against all odds reached a place of power and autonomy in our lives. We have to keep that, and we have to still use our voice no matter what.

Because the Cups are so much about emotional healing and fulfillment, there are times when the lessons of this Eight require hard work but are fairly simple. Queer clients of mine with PTSD or other related mental health concerns often pull this card as a sign to start trauma therapy. There are times when the Eight of Cups shows up earlier in our process of coming out and coming into our own as a card that urges you to keep leaving your old life (and identity) behind. What these things have in common is that they force us to do a deep dive into our emotional abyss. This is hard work, and you will feel weird in all of your relationships and across every area of your life. What you are leaving, though, is a time of buried emotions and unhealthy processing. What you'll come to is something so fulfilling and brilliant, you won't be able to believe you ever wanted to live in the pain for longer.

THE NINE AND TEN OF CUPS

The most common question I get asked in tarot classes is "What is the difference between the Nine and Ten of Cups?" There are a million different ways to answer this question, but I usually emphasize that Nines are about completion and Tens are about transformation. They both bring us happy, joyful conclusions regarding our love lives, families, and friendships. They're both excellent signs of substantial emotional healing. Those of us who are creative will see a lot of artistic success with either of these cards. The differences are subtle but they are important. The Nine merely completes our quest to find contentment, joy, or healing. Often called the Wish card, this card promises that whatever our watery heart wants, it can have right now. The Ten is more difficult but causes even more joy; this is a card of how love, friendship, and healing journeys change us. The Nine is about what's in our life at the end of these journeys, but the Ten is about who *we* are after going through the rest of the Cups cards.

Queering the Nine and Ten of Cups is really easy and really difficult because I see these cards as so innately queer as it is. The Ten even often features a giant rainbow!

Furthermore, if both of these cards are about following your heart until you reach a place of fulfillment and love, well, I don't know what's more queer than that. They show up for LGBTQQIP2SA+ seekers as promises, then. The Nine says that if we can endure countless Fives of Cups in our lives, learn to connect when we enter a Four of Cups phase, and cut through the crap in the Seven of Cups, we will be led here, to the Wish card. Whether we want a romantic partner or partners to grow old with, to find a polyamorous family enclave to slip right into happily, or just to find a career and group of friends that makes all of the hell we go through as marginalized people worth it, we will get there. This card promises that our needs are not too much, and that who we are is enough to be loved and supported. This card promises emotional healing no matter what you've been through. It's a card of completion, so one thing I've really found comforting from a healing perspective over the years is that the cycle of emotional healing *does* complete. I'm not going to be digging deep and overcoming myself for my entire life. At some point, this chapter will close, and I will move on to the next. In the next chapter, I will be happier, healthier, and even safer as a queer person.

The Ten ends our run of the Cups cards, though, reminding us that even when we're done, we're not. We have all of the information and tools we need, and it's up to us to use them regularly and transform ourselves and our lives into something beautiful. As LGBTQQIP2SA+ people, that can be something as straightforward as having figured out what makes us tick sexually and knowing how to embrace that for a happier life. It can mean enduring and working through enough therapy to have successful relationships with other radical LGBTQQIP2SA+ people, regardless of what we've been through.

Often, though, the Ten of Cups has us looking toward the future. We are basically promised relationships that transform us. We are certainly promised a period where we have healed enough to be a totally different person. How then, as empowered and supported queer people, do we carry that love into the world? How do we share it? What do we do with it? To me this card comes screaming as a reminder that my chosen family is for good. They have done the work of making me feel safe and secure in our familial love, and it is up to me to use that change in my life for the better. Often I get this card when what I need is time with these people that have helped me transform into someone trusting. This card also touches on the longevity we saw with the Ten of Pentacles. One of my greatest unfulfilled desires is to foster or house LGBTQQIP2SA+ children and teens who need that type of support. I'll know when the time is right, because the tarot will use the Ten of Cups to assure me that I have everything I need, and my life has evolved into one where I have plenty of love and resources to share.

It almost goes without saying, then, that the Ten of Cups is the one that shows up when queer people are ready to parent. It shows up when they're ready to start an arts organization. It shows up when they are ready to change careers to something involving caretaking or direct support. The Ten of Cups has a million different purposes, but queer seekers need to ask themselves only one question to get to the heart of it. "Now that my views of love and happiness have shifted, and now that so much of my journey to emotional healing has concluded . . . what do I want to do with that?"

QUEERING
THE
COURT CARDS

6

THE COURT CARDS

The court cards deserve their own section because so many tarot readers struggle to connect with them, and that's especially true of queer readers. It's easy to malign the court cards, but when you do crack them, they are some of the most informative and influential cards in the deck. I think talking about them as extensions of their suits as opposed to their own section of cards is part of the mistake in the learning curve, but it's also true that the cards themselves pose some problems in this day and age.

For those totally new to tarot, there are four court cards per suit. Traditionally, this is the Page or Knave, Knight, Queen, and King. If your deck is *Thoth* based—as is the *Urban Tarot*, which illustrates this book—they may be Princess, Prince, Queen, and Knight or some variation thereof. Modern decks do mix it up sometimes. Perhaps the most well-known change in the courts has been moving them from royalty to family roles, with daughter, son, mother, and father as the courts.

The Court Card system is inherently problematic from either a feminist or an LGBTQQIP2SA+ perspective. Assuming the King (or father, but we'll stick with the traditional ascriptions for now) as head of the suit is patriarchal at best, and we haven't even begun to delve into the heteronormativity of this. The court cards are one of the primary reasons I developed the *Queering the Tarot* series to begin with, and it's not hard to see why.

Queering the Queens and Kings of any suit can be tricky, and this is a point where a lot of students get caught up on their own path to learning tarot. The tarot, based on card order and the descriptions of the cards, does take a dated approach to these cards: the King is the head of the suit, whereas the Queen follows close behind but doesn't quite tap into that ultimate power. Furthermore, Queens are usually seen as the more emotional of the two, though more in-depth thought and knowing actual humans we ascribe to cards undo that a bit.

When I teach tarot, I teach three things to help us get around those trappings: The first is to learn these cards as energies, events, and pieces of advice first. *Then* you can go back and add elements of humanity and ascribe them to people. If students are ascribing only women to Queens and men to Kings, I make them scrap it and start over, using exclusively nonbinary or opposite-gender people that they know (or know of really well) to assign to each card. My cishet male best friend from college is clearly a Queen of Wands to me, which deepens my understanding of him and that card.

Finally, once we have four different ways to read the card and less gendered ideas of who represents each card, I ask students to look and see if they still think the King is the head of every suit. I personally usually shift the Queen of Cups to the head of that family. If Kings represent the peak of the card, all of that water emotion and sensitivity are going to create someone too emotional to run a kingdom! In the Wands I take a totally different approach. These cards are all about fight and fire and energy, and which court best represents that? Our Knight. Our fighter. So the Knight of Wands leads off that suit when I'm reading or ordering cards. In many queer spaces there is a move away entirely from hierarchies, and if it helps you to think of these four cards as totally interdependent and collaborative with *no one* in charge, then please feel free to do that. Recently in a class, a student suggested placing them in a circle, and not a line, so that each card's energy feeds off the next and there's no ending or beginning, so there's no head of the suit. I loved that and have been playing with it ever since.

One of the best ways to learn the court cards your own way is to think about what each title's role would be. Pages, for example, are messengers. Knights fight for the integrity of that suit's focus. Queens inspire and lead movements and nurture those in their kingdom. Kings teach and lead in more traditional ways. In focusing on the role, actions, and energies of the card, we start to lose both the heteronormativity and the cisnormativity of the traditional courts. We also allow our relationship to these cards to grow more naturally in line with how we've learned the rest of the tarot.

THE PAGE OF WANDS

In the tarot, Pages are usually considered messengers of the energy or events of the suit. That can also make them new ideas and sparks, or potential that hasn't begun to spread its wings yet. Traditionally then, the Page of Wands would indicate someone who brings new ideas and inspiration, or someone who has a lot of creative power festering inside them without a true outlet. The fire is there, but the Page hasn't quite learned how to make it their own. All of the Pages represent the potential of that

suit, but the potential of fire is even more powerful than this page realizes. Intuition, fervor, and so much more are running very deeply in a seeker who receives this card. The Page of Wands also indicates new creative ideas, new impulses coming from our gut instinct, and new passions or excitements coming to the surface. This Page can also indicate a sexual awakening on the horizon, regardless of one's identity. Fire is passion, creativity, and intuition. It's also sex. That gets lost in many conversations about the Wands, but it is a core function of their interpretations.

When queering the Page of Wands, we take everything we've already queered about the Wands, (social justice, queer identity as its own passion, and so on) and bring that into the idea of the Page as messenger. If the Page of Wands is showing up a lot, you could be looking at someone new to social justice or super fired-up about a cause you're looking to get involved with coming into your life. In a different type of queer reading, this is likely someone newly out or who has just found queer community or LGBTQQIP2SA+ friends for the first time. This card can also indicate someone starting a path of activism, likely the querent.

That fire and spark for all things queer are fresh, new, and often contagious (in a good way) when someone is finding their footing in the LGBTQQIP2SA+

community. When looking at this interpretation of the Page as an energy, the cards are urging *you* to find new inspiration as someone who creates positive change in the world. This card is a wake-up call, and meant to help you identify that yearning that hasn't had a home as one of queer activism. Alternatively, that creative spark still exists and is potentially amplified in a queer telling of this card—specifically you may be called to put more of yourself and your identity into upcoming creative projects.

The Pages often come up when people are asking about their sexual or gender identity (and, uncomfortably, when they aren't but are open to hearing "anything the cards have to say"). In these cases the querent is either still in the closet or hasn't gotten truly comfortable yet. Their identity may also be shifting. In any of these cases, if it's a question of sexual identity, the seeker is likely to meet someone soon who will be able to stoke that fire and make them feel more impassioned about really living as that identity (whatever that looks like to the seeker—there is no exact blueprint for queerness). In short, an important fling or short-term, decidedly queer relationship is on its way. If it's a question of gender identity, it's a little different. The querent has likely been out and transitioning or even living as their true gender for a short time. Often in these cases it's a matter of trial and error to see what makes them feel comfortable in their skin, and the Page of Wands indicates really coming into one's own in that regard. Once we feel that way, we start to love and forgive ourselves, and self-love is an important fire to build and nurture, too.

Finally, the Page of Wands serves to remind us that social and political change are always happening. While this is true across identities, for LGBTQQIP2SA+ people this is often an important acknowledgment when we are feeling frustrated or stuck, whether that means stuck in a town where we can't meet anyone, stuck in a job with a transphobic employer, or stuck in our own bodies trying to figure out how to navigate and feel comfortable in them. Of course, if surrounded by negative cards, this page can be a warning that new fire is needed because the fight for justice could become a lot harder. That's a type of social change too, and a crucial application of a queer Page of Wands that I don't want to overlook. This is ultimately a positive card, though, so that fight, that spark, that fire is settled deep inside of you somewhere. Whether you've been fighting the good fight for one week or one decade, the Page promises that you have even more to give. It's still a card of potential, no matter how far along on our path we think we are. Again, the Page reminds us that change is coming, and it doesn't make a judgment on what that looks like, so if surrounded by or crossed by positive cards this Page is a welcome confirmation that things are about to blow up for us and our community in a big, beautiful, blazing way.

THE KNIGHT OF WANDS

If I had to sum up the entire suit of Wands in one card, this is the suit where it wouldn't be the King, Queen, or even the Ace. Sure, those cards have their own importance and symbolize intense fire, but nothing screams "fire, fight, and passion" like the Knight. Knights are warriors, after all, battling intensely for the things and people they've sworn fealty to. The Knight of Wands is a shining example of that adventurous spirit, lust for life, and desire for change so typical in a Wands card. Even when we look at the downfall of a suit built on fire and gut instinct, the Knight upholds those archetypes to a T too. This Knight, for all their zest and good intent, often burns out, losing interest or expending too much energy too quickly. They're impulsive, and while they're the person you want around for the launch of your new project, don't expect them to be there at the end. The Knight of Wands loves a hot pursuit, and in fact, one may be on the horizon for you—but the pursuit and the chase are often all this Knight has in them. This applies when it's an energy manifesting in your own life, too. You may find yourself full of piss and vinegar one day, and completely over it or exhausted the next.

As advice, the Knight of Wands pushes you to experiment with a new passion or adventure, but warns that your own lack of follow-through could squash your chances of long-term success. As an event, they rush in, inspiring and creating change quickly. The Knight of Wands might be a succession of wins, a sudden collapse of something that was holding other things back, or one big opportunity that you've got to grab and ride for all it's worth. In any case, they rush in bringing big ideas, fully equipped to start a wildfire.

As we've looked at queering the tarot, and how wands represent our social justice movements, the Knight translates easily to people we all know and love. Harvey

Milk was a Knight of Wands if I've ever seen one, as was Marsha P. Johnson. When you need to start a revolution through politics or riot, the Knight of Wands is at the forefront breaking down those doors for you. Like any court card, this card can represent the querent in question or someone new and powerful entering your world. I would argue that in either case you're being encouraged to take on that energy, either of your own accord or in emulation of the third party.

The Knight of Wands can also represent social movements themselves. Stonewall was a Knight of Wands, quickly changing the course of LGBTQQIP2SA+ futures, though not lasting long in and of itself. The dark side of the Knight of Wands shows that while I often speak highly of fire, its nature is inherently destructive. The AIDS epidemic of the '80s could arguably be considered a Knight of Wands. While its time frame was a lot longer than is typical for this card, the way it wreaked havoc so quickly and left permanent scars that our community cannot erase still screams Knight of Wands.

That's another important element of the Knight of Wands: once fire has started, there's often no stopping it, and with the Knight flaming fully, all potential and instinct, it leaves lasting—often permanent—damage in its wake. Which means that, while the queer community can use this card's energy to smash the patriarchy and open new doors for LGBTQQIP2SA+ kids, there's a lesson in here too to watch our backs for Knights with different agendas and loyalties sneaking in behind us.

The Knight of Wands shows up in our microcosms, too. For many young querents who have recently come out, it heralds the immense passion and lust that can come with first queer love. Someone is likely rushing into this person's life to sweep them totally off their feet, and yes, after the process of coming out and all of its ups and downs, the querent deserves every bit of excitement and passion and joy this Knight can bring. That same warning still stands, though. Often clients of all identities come asking about their current relationship, receive this card, and aren't too thrilled to see that lack of follow-through. So while this card brings all the highs of new queer love that the Netflix LGBTQ channel promises us, it can also bring news of dire heartbreak at the end. Even so, I will usually encourage seekers to pursue and ride this out for everything they can. LGBTQQIP2SA+ people spend most of our lives being told we should be ashamed of our sexuality, that it is too big, too dangerous, too brazen. This is a harmful and dangerous message. Everyone deserves good sex and to honor themselves in that way, and as long as you can handle that this isn't a forever person, this Knight is a strong sign to go for it.

The Knight of Wands applies to anything that we're passionate about and affected deeply by. For queer seekers this can also include pursuit of a chosen family, artistic expression, alternative spiritual paths, and so much more. These are things LGBTQQIP2SA+ people often need as part of their healing from societal or familial oppression and struggle, and the intensity and burning they bring into our lives at first is often the first time we feel alive since we began choking down our emotions regarding our treatment and history. When that pursuit ends or the fire dies down to a manageable level (or blows out entirely), or when it blooms into something so large and out of control we couldn't have foreseen it, it leaves a stinging numbness that makes us question if we'll feel that again (or whether we should ever have pursued it in the first place).

In readings for non-queer seekers, the Knight of Wands often brings primarily good things (just with some warnings), but when you've been marginalized or traumatized, that sudden cold leaves every bit the scar being burned does. In these cases, I pull some additional cards for healing, or to show the seeker where they can still find that fire, be it in themselves or through external sources. This is a card that, because of its quick, urgent, but ultimately transient, pursuit-oriented nature, often can't be read alone—especially when we're dealing with deeper issues.

The Knight of Wands packs a powerful fiery punch no matter what. While I don't shy away from the negativity in this card, most LGBTQQIP2SA+ people are eager for sudden, substantial change, and when wielded with another weapon (perhaps one aimed at longevity and foresight), the energy of this card allows us to be a messenger and an agent of that very change. This is a card that promises adventure and sensuality, excitement and power. For all marginalized people, this card reminds us that these things, too, are a part of life that we are entitled to, and that through these ideas we regain and reclaim our power. It's a call to remember that no matter how many times the fire in this card blows out, we are fully capable of picking it up again, and a reminder that should things get out of control . . . well, that was probably what was supposed to happen anyway. Just don't run away leaving the next person in line to clean up your mess.

THE QUEEN OF WANDS

The Queen of Wands, too, is fire itself—determined, dominant, and demanding—a great leader with a lot of compassion and passion for change, but a fierce punch in the gut if you're part of the problem they're trying to fix. As an energy, this is determination and dominance. As advice, this card tells you to plow ahead no matter what, being as bold and take-charge as you need to be to accomplish your goal. As an event, you should welcome and relish opportunities for leadership or to take the reins. This Queen is usually an extroverted energy, gregarious and generous. Queen bees of all genders who are actually kind often have this Queen of Wands energy, and real life Queens of Wands are some of my favorite people on the planet. This Queen is busy and active and loves to hustle. As a result they're popular and in demand, but will make time for everything and everyone that's important to them. The Queen of Wands is also stubbornness and will resort to deception or flat-out bullying to win once they've dug their fabulous heels in. While those are technically considered shortcomings, I usually admire their work and drive even in these instances. This energy *is* fire, so it's also a quick temper, passion that moves and changes easily, and sex.

Which brings us to our first segment on further queering this card. This card is sex. It's also dominance. I've read for straight women and a few men hitting an unexpected sexual peak later in life where this card comes up, but I see it most often for sexual minorities hitting those same peaks. This is a time when you don't want to settle down, and your primary objective is sex. This is a positive card, so that's great. Go, spread your fire (but be safe). If this card comes up repeatedly, it's time to look at that dominant side of your personality that you probably aren't using in the bedroom the way you could be. There are either tangible skills that go into being a dominant or an actual acknowledgment and grabbing of that energy that you haven't reckoned with, but this card in a reading about relationships or sex is urging you to get those skills you feel you're lacking.

The Queen of Wands represents a high sex drive, but it also represents having a lot of fire and passion to give beyond just sex. If that is the case and you're repeatedly getting this card about love or relationships, it may be time to look at non-monogamous options in your personal life as well. As we think about queering the tarot and therefore the world and institutions around us, relationships can look like anything we want them to when we find compatible partners. You don't have to give your whole self to one person if that isn't something you are capable of, believe in, or are able to do without overwhelming them or wearing them out.

The other major aspect of the Queen of Wands ties back to the topic of creating change and furthering social justice movements that the entire Wands suit addresses. These natural leaders are often brilliant community organizers and genius strategists. They might not have thrown the first brick at Stonewall, but they did lead and organize the ensuing riot. They're not Knights. They're not fighters. Yet without a Queen of Wands sitting at the helm, you're not likely to get much done. If you repeatedly receive the Queen of Wands, it's probably time to pick a cause and get cracking, either developing an organization where there isn't one, or stepping into a leadership position in an existing situation.

The Queen of Wands can come up easily next to the Ten of Wands, our card of burnout and overwork when I'm reading for activists. This happens almost weekly. The Queen loves to be busy and is also stubborn, so they will often ignore their own limits and boundaries to accomplish change, then end up collapsing in exhaustion and irritation. For extroverts like this Queen, this is an easy fix—a night out with friends where the work and the collective are not points of conversation. In truth these Queens like anything sensual, so a night of dancing, good wine, and gossip in a queer setting will get them right back on their feet. Sometimes, though, we are legitimately burned out and need to rest, so look closely at your other cards to make sure you're not overlooking signs of this.

Finally, if this card is fire (and it is) then it is also gut instinct. As queer people, we often spend a lot of time denying our own truths, usually for more years than we've been trying to live in those truths. Which means even if we are currently the most out and proud person that ever existed, we have spent so much time denying what our gut was screaming at us, that things sitting in that instinct like "change jobs," "move to Ohio," or, hell, "start eating better" get shut down and overlooked. We don't know how to trust this feeling. We don't know how to trust ourselves. This Queen lives and thrives in that instinct and urges you to do the same. When there are decisions to make, take some incredibly deep, long breaths, and then do a body check. How do you feel physically? Where do you need to pay more attention to yourself? Finally, what is the answer to that question that's been bugging you? It's in there.

THE KING OF WANDS

In the first tarot deck I truly learned to read, the King of Wands sits on his throne looking excited, determined, and kind. This kindness, which is actually not as common in other decks, has colored my entire relationship with this card and this version of that fiery Wands energy. The King of Wands is a natural born leader, but whereas the Queen often leads with dominance and creativity, the King leads with kindness and almost seems like he's letting you in on a secret as he encourages you to change the world with him. This King is very honorable and will never crack his own idealistic code. As an event, the King symbolizes those moments when we learn that wrecking the system requires working with the system, at least for a time—though never through cheating or manipulating our way in. As an energy, this King is every bit the raw fire that the Queen is, just applied differently. This King in any format likes challenges and will often argue just to win, though I personally read even that trait with a touch of cheekiness to it. Speaking of cheeky, this King loves a practical joke and has a true lust for life when it comes to anything that inspires big belly laughs.

When queering the tarot, the King and Queen have quite a bit in common. They are both natural leaders in social justice movements. They are both strong lovers, and they both lack the follow-through one would hope for in an otherwise great leader or partner. There are some substantial differences, though, especially when we see the kindness and mischief in this King. Whereas the Queen tirelessly organizes and leads our social justice movements in the margins where the rest of us are, the King likes to play diplomat, actually going out and having hard conversations about political bills that are advancing or breaking down racism in one-on-one conversations with people. He works tirelessly, too, and is always willing to do the crucial emotional labor that many of us in the activist or LGBTQQIP2SA+ don't have the energy for. As a major face card in the fiery suit of Wands, his passion for community and justice run every bit as deep as the Queen's. In addition to having those hard conversations, this King is also the community leader who throws potluck dinners so we can all come together and is often seen heading up arts groups doing important work. Crucial fighting for marginalized people's rights and dignities happens in marches, courtrooms, and in the streets—but it happens elsewhere, too. It happens in theatres, in conversations with high school friends, at brunches with co-workers. That's where you'll find the King of Wands working to open people's hearts and minds.

Outside of his activist work, you'll find Kings of Wands of all genders at the bar after hours looking for bossy lovers. While this King isn't a bottom per se, he loves the back-and-forth that comes with meeting other fiery people and taking them home. Like the Queen, he's incredibly sex-driven, but whereas she likes to command and be followed, he just wants to have a good time. He's willing to let you win those bedroom brawls if that sounds the most fun, but he's hoping you're a switch, too. As a romantic partner, the King has a little bit easier time with monogamy than the Queen—if your intellectual and physical connections are compelling enough, that is. That being said, if the King keeps coming up in readings when you're struggling with monogamy, you might want to think about your own drives and desires and how important non-monogamy may actually be to you. Even if you're in a relationship and choose not to open it, knowing you're a polyamorous or non-monogamous person choosing to act monogamously is a completely different experience from believing you, left to your own devices, are monogamous. However, whereas the Queen often feels best with multiple partners, the King is often just as happy with one solid partner and occasional flings or one-night stands. The kink community on the whole is recognized in this card, so we might not get *submissive* or *dominant* from this card alone, but we do know you need a little more driving your carnal life than others may be happy with.

I've touched on how queering this card can often mean arts leadership, and that is more true in the queer community than elsewhere. An LGBTQQIP2SA+ person coming in for a reading who feels unsatisfied by their job situation is likely craving raw creativity and *true art,* even if they can't define the latter. Arts leadership is where much of our queer advocacy and community-building happens, and I would strongly encourage such a person to organize an open mic or try curating a show or directing a play to satisfy that nagging feeling that there is something *more.* Because this card is gut instinct and creativity but is also natural leadership skills, they make perfect artistic directors, art dealers, and creative producers in any medium they hone in on. As mentioned with the Queen of Wands, queer people are so often told that our gut instinct is wrong, and learning to overcome that coding and speak out is liberating. Someone with King of Wands energy will learn to use that freeing feeling to create artistic opportunities for others to do the same. This is just conjecture, but I believe that's why LGBTQQIP2SA+ people specifically make great arts leaders when receiving the King of Wands card often in their readings.

Then there is that pesky piece about the gut instinct. When used like the Queen of Wands, we overcome all of those years of being told our gut instinct about ourselves and our desires is not enough or straight up that we're not good enough, and we become masters of trusting our gut over time. However, a King of Wands, as that more playful side of fire personified, may start losing control, relying on gut instincts and urges (and happily conflating the two) instead of applying logic or emotion to the situation. While this is always a concern for someone who regularly receives the King of Wands in readings, for an LGBTQQIP2SA+ person who spent years denying this instinct and believing it was wrong, there is extra danger in losing control when we start trying to own that part of ourselves. The King of Wands can bring a strong reassurance that trusting your gut is right and safe and good—but it can also bring a quick warning. Our gut instinct's concern is keeping us safe in the moment. It doesn't care where we want to be in five, ten, or fifteen years. Which does mean that it isn't always right. When it's telling you not to trust someone you just met, or that maybe you shouldn't spend that extra $200 on new shoes, you should definitely listen to it. If it's telling you to burn down the things in your life that you love because of a self-destructive coping mechanism that you developed as a closeted queer person? You probably shouldn't listen to that. Self-destruction is very present in the King of Wands. Fire is beautiful, and creative, and it burns unnecessary things to the ground. It's also dangerous and easy to lose control of. The challenge of this card is learning that balance. Learning to temper your moods, your gut urges, or your raw fire is crucial for a King of Wands—or for someone receiving the card frequently in readings.

THE PAGE OF SWORDS

The Page of Swords normally stands proudly but hesitantly holding a sword while looking either toward or away from the action of the rest of the card. As a person, this Page is normally young or new on their path. Pages are messengers, and the Swords are our cards of logic, cool heads, mental health, and recovering from oppression or trauma. Writers frequently get Sword court cards, as do doctors, mathematicians, and scientists. The Page of Swords as an energy delivers new insight or clarity regarding tense circumstances, illuminates new ways of healing or coping, or brings a new type of thought and energy. The Sword cards are action-oriented once there's a plan. The Page is ready to wield that Sword, as long as they know what they're doing. As advice, you are likely being called to contribute fresh thought and critical planning to a situation, or perhaps you're being told that you have a plan already, so it's time to take charge and act. As an event, you are likely entering a period of new ideas or insights into your own life, or this is a period where you're learning a lot of new information. The Page of Swords is critically honest and forever curious about the *why* of any given situation. All of the Swords court cards represent a time to cut away negative habits, relationships, or situations. The Page is a good bit kinder than the rest of these court cards, so if that's the message that comes through in a reading, this is likely a mutual decision, a habit that's died off already, or something you can gently wean yourself off of.

The Page of Swords has shown up often for me since I started my tarot journey in a dusty dorm room basement a decade and a half ago. Quite frankly, once I realized I was queer, this card showed up again and again and again to push me to just get it over with and come out. Even if you are already out to the world at large, this card indicates a need to come out at work, to your grandparent, or wherever that hole in honesty lies. The Page is not a negative card, so it's safe to come out now.

Alternatively, the Page of Swords also speaks to sexual and gender fluidity. Many of us come out as one thing, with a specific understanding of ourselves or our identity. As that shifts and evolves, the Page of Swords will show up to urge you to live your truth, however fleeting or confusing that truth may be. Words are important to Sword cards; there are many other cards that deal with fluidity where you don't have to call yourselves anything, but with a Page of Swords, labels can be affirming and freeing. This card, then, urges you to seek a label that fits your current experience. As your sexual identity shifts and grows, the Page of Swords will probably show up each time—not only as that annoying tough-love friend promising you that all of this was safe to feel, discuss, and live as, but also pushing you to accept yourself in all of your various iterations. The Page of Swords will call you to face any changes you're going through instead of running away or doubling down on identities that no longer fit you.

While Wands deal more directly with social justice action than I often see the Swords doing, this Page *is* a call to action. We've spent this whole suit dealing with oppression, and we spent the Wands suit learning to harness our fire into something actionable. Now the Page of Swords shows up to assure us that all of this planning has paid off and that we are ready to pick up a Sword and fight. This is most likely a head-on battle. The Swords do represent law, medicine, and related careers, but this is not fighting from within or trying to create change while also holding a job in one of these offices. The Page wants you to prepare for a battle—you versus the person or organization you've been struggling with. You are ready.

We've talked a lot about the Swords in regards to mental health and healing from trauma. This Page brings a kind-but-urgent cool-headedness, as you realize it's time to bring in a professional to help you through your next stages of healing. You need psychological insight that doing the work on your own will no longer provide, but you're also ready and feeling equipped to do the deep work that any good therapist will require of you. It is not only spiritually safe to move to another plane of coping or healing, but also emotionally safe to dig deep and accept third-party insight. In some cases, this card could indicate that mental health medication is needed now. You're either starting a cycle of mental illness again or are coming out of one, and the Page of Swords shows up because they just want you to feel better this time around.

As we look at the world around us right now, it's so easy to feel completely over-whelmed and frustrated. Many of us are dealing with really deep cases of compassion fatigue, disassociation, or blatant exhaustion from trying to handle everything. The Page of Swords also seems to be evolving to adapt to these times. I'm seeing people who have never struggled with mental illness before needing to seek therapy or to learn coping mechanisms. I'm seeing some of the most well-balanced people I've ever met start to spin out. These are difficult, trying times. The Page of Swords shows up to remind you of the reality of the situation, both good and bad. Yes, this oppression that the Swords often deal with is very real. It's not all coming from institutions this time either; homes are being destroyed from natural disasters and we are left literally picking up the debris, often without the aid of the people and places we are supposed to trust to help us.

The Page of Swords is not going to lie to you about the reality we are facing—however, it does bring a new view. Part of queering anything is learning alternative ways of existing, loving, and thriving. If we can't rely on a government agency to give us an opportunity to help, we can find a new way to aid those in need. We can form a new organization, send what's needed to individuals we know how to reach, or get together to brainstorm totally new ways of putting our passion into action. Ultimately, this is what the Page of Swords wants us to do, and it's what too much of the world needs from us now. The old ways are broken, and they might not be fixable. Find a new way. If that, too, fails, *be* a new way.

THE KNIGHT OF SWORDS

If Swords is our suit of air, logic, and communication, the Knight is a fighter who will do whatever it takes to be heard and make sure you are, too. The Knight is direct, analytical, and not afraid of a long battle, a hard journey, or a war of words. However, this is a card that represents air in its truest form, which means this Knight can be coldly logical, to the point of being unfeeling. Paired with the fast action of the Swords suit, that can mean that as soon as we're accustomed to this Knight's confident ways and are rebuilding after they've turned our world upside down with their insight, they're often gone, leaving us alone to clean up the debris. This makes them players and heartbreakers in traditional tarot, or destructive friends and co-workers in modern day. They are opinionated to a fault when badly aspected, and not afraid to crush you by sharing their opinion. As an energy, this disruptive influence in a suit that deals so much with mental health can show crushing relapses after a period of good health or sobriety. On the flip side, if you've been avoiding the reality of a situation in your life—be it your mental health or anything else—this Knight is a needed wake-up call.

As we look at this card from the perspective of an LGBTQQIP2SA+ querent, we see both the best and worst of this card double back on us. First, the negative: if this card is harsh words or hateful actions, then warnings of bigotry or hatred from where you least expect it could be present. I have seen this card show up as a seeker's mom verbally attacking them over dinner, seemingly out of the blue, as losing friends upon coming out, and as job losses because someone's name got linked to activist work they were doing. This card can be dangerous, and for those of us who are statistically more likely to face danger, that's especially true. There's something, too, about the specific nature of the Knight of Swords that screams "danger from where we least expect it," which can indicate the abuse and harassment that

176

do happen within the queer community. If you've just met someone new and this card comes up—run. That's true for non-queer seekers too, but it's important to take the statistical likelihood of a queer person being victimized into account when you are reading for an LGBTQQIP2SA+ person.

When looking at the statistical likelihood of a queer person facing trauma, this includes the sides of the card that deal with sobriety and mental illness. Statistically, these issues disproportionately affect LGBTQQIP2SA+ people, and the Knight of Swords very often indicates relapse. What's worse is that this card often indicates relapse without resources to help you. This is something that crashes in and wrecks everything you tried to build, and leaves you wondering what happened with nowhere to turn. In cases of those dealing with sobriety and mental health, the warning comes so you can gather a list of resources in advance or try to avoid this pitfall altogether. Get your wellness tool kit together, and rely heavily on that until you feel in your gut that the dangerous time has passed.

Then there's the positive. This card can be a beautiful call to action and a powerful source of encouragement and affirmation to our community in ever-trying political times. This Knight knows how to use language and communication to open doors and create real transformation where others have failed. This Knight will fight until there is no fighting left to do. This Knight storms into workplaces and works from within to change the company's model to a more LGBTQQIP2SA+ inclusive one. This Knight takes meetings with senators and argues with them until they're blue in the face for fair legislation. Knights of Swords are pillars in communities that are starving for equity and acceptance. They aren't nice, and they don't deal well with tone policing. They shouldn't. They are able to use their words to educate and force change through the academic language that intimidates queerphobic people. If this card is coming up in a reading, you are being called to pull your resources together to stake your case, and if that doesn't work, to shake things up through any means necessary. This Knight might be cutting and smart—but their most important attribute is that they get the job done. I mentioned before that this Knight crashes in and wrecks everything you tried to build, but when someone is building something on a pillar of patriarchy, white supremacy, or heteronormativity, that's exactly who you want to be.

THE QUEEN OF SWORDS

The Queen of Swords is most often depicted sitting on a throne looking regal and proud. This archetypal figure is often seen or understood to be an older, independent woman—often a widow who has done just fine on her own. She wields the Sword calmly and confidently with a look on her face that lets you know she will use this tool when needed. This Queen tells it like it is, values honesty, and is a quick thinker with almost supernatural perception. This means she's not only concerned with what is fair and just, but also is a master at sussing out what's really going on. She is intelligent and strong, and able to make absolute judgments devoid of emotion. She does not lack compassion or personality, though, and usually errs on the side of what is truly just. Traditionally that means this card is read either as a person in the querent's life that fits that description, or as an energy that the querent is being called to take on. If you're asking about basic life decisions, this card is telling you to make either the most logical decision, or perhaps the one that honors yourself the most. If you're dealing with problematic or troubling people in an area of your life, the Queen of Swords is telling you to be compassionate but to consider wielding the sword to sever those ties. This Queen always wants you to be honest with yourself and others when making your decisions, and to do so independently.

The Queen of Swords, to me, brings two images to mind. One of is of my queer-platonic partner's grandmother, and that is perhaps why I see so much compassion and love in this card despite its seemingly cold appearance. The Queen of Swords isn't cruel and is actually a bit of a marshmallow. She's not going to mince words, though, and she's going to expect you to pull yourself together when it's time to get things done. What this brings to mind from a queer perspective is the question

"What do we owe our community?" Self-care is important, but so is the work we're doing. I am absolutely not telling you not to live in or express your neuroatypicality or to just get over any trauma you've experienced. When you've committed to a social justice movement or a project that will help your community, though, there is, unfortunately, a time where you *do* just have to pull yourself together and get stuff done. Whether you haven't been behaving like your best self or just haven't been putting your promised energy in, this card shows up to remind you that now is the time to get a grip on yourself and go back out there and fight. There are other cards in the deck that let you know when you are too sick (mentally or physically) to continue, like the Ten of Wands. This Queen is pushing you to stand back up and get back to it.

Alternatively, this card also shows up when you've been doing no self-care whatsoever. If you've been fighting and working and putting in a ton of emotional labor for other people, the Queen of Swords shows up to remind you that you can pull back and cool off for a bit. However, self-care isn't always rest and coloring. How clean is your home? How clean are *you*? Have you been eating and drinking enough water lately? Have you been sleeping? As the Swords so often do, this card delivers the advice we don't always want but do need. It might seem contradictory to include both messages, but really this Queen shows up to dish out the advice you need the most when you need it the most. Surrounding cards are important, but so is having a longer conversation with the seeker, especially if that seeker is you.

The Queen of Swords is often the marker of a queer woman in general for me. I often try to stay away from the gendered assignations in the tarot unless it's to subvert them, but the other image this card calls to mind for me is the Virgin archetype of yesteryear, that is, a woman who is independent, unmarried, a happy Old Maid. After years of scholarly research, we know that a great number of these women were LGBTQQIP2SA+ without the language or public acceptance to be out as such. Despite being in the closet, the ones we know about regularly spoke out against the society they lived in, using their wits or their pens to create scathing critiques of their times. This is incredibly representative of the Queen of Swords; her own identity sits close to her chest, but she will be damned if she won't speak out on the injustice others are facing.

The Queen of Swords speaks deeply to the part of our wounded radical souls that still thinks that in the end justice will win out. We want to be this person who so firmly but lovingly commands this sword, using our words for good and allowing that good to win out. It isn't always a realistic message, but it's an important one. What is truly just and truly fair *can* win. We can speak out against oppression in our society and become Queen. We can create the world we want to see through fighting or creating or whatever else we have at our disposal. In my heart, I still believe those things are true even as we lose battle after battle in the present day. Yet we keep fighting, and when we want to stop, the Queen of Swords shows up to say, "No, keep going." This card is the energy that drives us toward fairness and equality no matter what. This card knows the only way to win is with strength and confidence, and it shows up when the message that those things matter is precisely what we need to hear.

THE KING OF SWORDS

Contrary to the Queen of Swords, the King is often seen as lacking compassion. This is someone so intellectually driven that the only thing they can see is that their way is the right way. This is someone so eager to rule, they will gladly step on other people to get there. This King is peak Air—cool, callous, and so sure that what they are doing is for the greater good that they're willing to rule out empathy. This King is not *all* bad, though—very few things in the world are strictly good or bad, right or wrong. If you need to make a decision for *you*, this card shows up urging you to think about your own best interests and cut away anything that is unnecessary or damaging to you in the process. We sometimes need a shot of intellect to remind us not to get totally lost in a rush of feelings or passion. It can also be a warning—this King doesn't care about our feelings, but if something that inhibits the greater good is coming, they're going to tell us. This card can very easily be about clarity and finding peace. It can also tell you to own your power in a given situation. It even has wonderful affirmations for those considering new technology or medical care. With this King, those things are incredibly well aspected.

This is still one of my least favorite cards to get in a reading. I don't like being selfish, even when I know it's for the best. I don't like conflict or fighting, even when they're necessary. All of this does make the King of Swords one of the most interesting to queer, though. This King can be and often is so obviously white supremacist patriarchy. This is the world and the set of institutions that are so cruel to LGBTQQ-IP2SA+ people or anyone who is marginalized. This card in a reading often says, "You're not wrong—fighting this is going to suck, and you might lose," or it says, "Well, you were on a good trajectory, but now this sexist or transphobic thing is going to mess it all up." This sword in this King's hand might be coming for you, or you might find out that the things you're grappling with are because the sword has already swung in your direction. This is why it is one of my least favorite cards, and I have seen it manifest this a dozen times in the past couple of years especially.

Yet this King's Sword is double edged, and like most (if not all) of the Swords cards, there are ways we can still win against whatever it is we are facing or fighting. While so much of my work queering the tarot with LGBTQQIP2SA+ clients is centered on following your heart and listening to your gut, when we are in the thick of a fight that unfortunately doesn't always work on its own, sometimes we need to think like our oppressor, using a clear head and an aggressive energy and succinct and intellectual communication to open someone's mind or even to beat them in a court of law. Sometimes we need to be willing to pick up that Sword and say, "Hey, you—I'm done. I'm cutting this down"—whether that *this* is a rule or law we don't agree with and decide to fight, or a person's effect and influence on our life.

The King of Swords rarely ends totally happily. In fact, it rarely ends. You might change that law but the system is still slanted against you. You might open someone's mind but what about the next fifty people? You might win the battle, but the war for your dignity and your rights is still raging. That's okay. This card teaches us how to fight, and that's important whether we're winning that fight or not. In fact, it's crucial. We need to know how to walk the talk if we want to survive in our society. The Tower promises big, dramatic change, but the little-by-little and step-by-step are just as crucial to creating real and sustaining change, and that's what the King of Swords can bring if we let them. Not everything terrible that happens has a higher purpose. Humans have free will, and humans cause most of the awful things in this world with that free will. We can choose to use our own free will to learn from these experiences anyway, to sharpen our swords, hone our fight skills, and eventually, cut it all down.

THE PAGE OF PENTACLES

If the Page of Pentacles comes up in a reading, you likely have big dreams and are fully capable of manifesting them. Loads of people get this card when they're considering starting their own business, building a house, or moving across the country. We are still young and new on our path with this card, and this messenger shows up urging us to take chances—albeit smart, well-measured chances—to make those dreams come true. I mention the smart, well-measured path here because the Pentacles are all about practicality and stability. You'll want a business plan, a blueprint, or a road map and a savings account when you're looking at making those big changes. The potential in your life when this card shows up is astronomical, though. Aim to start your own business, and you'll wind up in *Forbes* some day. Aim to build a house and find yourself creating a home and a legacy. Decide to move across the country, and let adventure untold find you. This card is a positive omen for students, with an educational path laid out and a shining future once they graduate.

This Page often shows up when people are newly out of the closet, although often when they have some other degree of privilege such as a supportive family or a high-paying job that is queer-friendly. The road ahead shows a lot to learn, and there are many queer experiences you'll want to get under your belt, but it is a positive road ahead. Often it shows up once some other processes we've seen thus far in the Pentacles play out. Maybe you weren't safe or promised a smooth road ahead at one point, but now have your plans, your optimism, and the karmic energy working in your favor to forge ahead. Maybe you scraped and scrambled for years, and are ready to start something new. In any case, this Page promises no material hiccups and that you'll be able to create a nice life for the real, actual you.

This is a card where issues of queer parenting arise—likely an LGBTQQIP2SA+ person looking to become a parent and being promised that their chosen method will allow them to create the family they want. Unfortunately, with this card's orientation toward material goods, you might have to invest a little to make that dream of queer parenting a reality, but it will happen. This is so often true of queer parenting anyway—not only do we need the resources it takes to raise a child (like everyone does), but also, using methods like in vitro fertilization or adoption to create a family burden us with extra costs. This is a positive card, though, so while the money involved in this process may not be ideal, it is well aspected. You won't go without, and you will get to start your family soon.

As this is a suit that, when queered, becomes about community, one of my favorite manifestations of the Page is when communities start growing. In Minneapolis, Minnesota, where I have lived for a decade, there used to be just a handful of queer events and spaces. Still, it was substantially better than where I grew up, even when some of those event-planning companies folded and a few of our spaces went under. After a couple of years, though, we hit a Page of Pentacles moment. Dance nights started popping up in spaces we didn't expect, and now we can choose between a number of queer-led arts events or dining options on any given night. Before we could get there, though, we had to recover from the previous slew of options shutting down, and celebrate and revel in the strength of those that remained steadfast for us in those times. If this card shows up regarding your hometown or need for community, don't worry. The roots you need will start growing around you—you just have to find them and make sure you're a part of it all.

THE KNIGHT OF PENTACLES

To be honest, this is not my favorite card in the deck. Don't get me wrong. This Knight is kind, hardworking, and destined to be successful in their own way. Yet read or looked at traditionally, this card has always bored me. Being methodical is great, but I want to know about my end goal, not sit there stewing in the method it takes to get there. I am all about hard work, but if it's tedious and not stimulating me mentally, emotionally, or physically, I would rather bang my head against the keyboard than deal with it. However, this card, for all of its frustrating messages about towing the line and continuing to work where you are, is necessary. It makes the dreams of the Page a reality and gives us all a firm foundation to stand on.

In every project, we have to come to this point sometime. In every community, we would get nowhere without the community members who do the data entry at our favorite nonprofits. That person entering the data? Their long-term dream of running that nonprofit would never come true if they didn't get their foot in the door somewhere. So this Knight shows up to give us strength when we don't want to do that work anywhere. When queering this card, it could be time to send a thank you card to the people doing tireless, less glitzy work in the LGBTQQIP2SA+ community where you live. It could be reminding us that every right and dignity we have is because someone was willing to do that work. Not every act of revolution is fire and fighting. It might seem ironic, then, for this Knight, this fighter, to be the one to remind us that while some of our freedom was won with war, some of it was won by trying over and over again (in the court system, for example) until the tide turned. Some of it was won because someone ran for office and then came out. Some of it was won because someone who related a lot to this Knight went from house to house having endless hard conversations with friends and family who weren't as enlightened. There are all kinds of ways to fight, and this Knight takes a practical approach that earns them and their community one step forward at a time until, eventually, they reach that finish line.

In the literal fighter and Earth interpretations, this Knight could be someone who works to make sure their community is provided for practically. If you're looking for a calling, this card could be telling you to go into housing development focusing on lower-income homes for people who are marginalized, or it could be telling you to pick a vocation rooted in making sure the basic needs of trans people are met. In its simplest queer form, this card could be telling you to open up your own home or heart to an LGBTQQIP2SA+ friend who needs it, allowing your own solid foundation to help someone else. Your immediate chosen family (any chosen family you live with) is likely taken care of thanks to your hard work and diligence creating that home or space, and now it's time to think about what you have to offer the queer community at large.

THE QUEEN OF PENTACLES

The Queen of Pentacles is most often depicted as a confident and wealthy presumed-woman who is a good mother and a disciplined worker, and manages to squeeze time for luxury and enjoying herself in there, too. In many ways this card epitomizes the goal of work/life balance. This Queen makes it look easy, whether she's tending to work, family, her investments, or the beautiful and soft things she's bought herself to be comfortable in. This card is almost always a good sign when you're asking about business or money, but it's a good omen for home life, too. I've seen this card come up often when clients ask about advancing at work, especially if they're considering taking on a leadership role. I've seen it come up countless times for parents who are worried about what kind of people their kids would become as they aged, and it's a sure sign that your side of the work in raising your family is nearing an end and you can be confident in what happens next. I see this card most often when people are looking to invest or retire. It essentially screams, "Yes!" if you're asking questions about whether you should, but it paves a path of confidence and warm energy if you're looking for the how or where.

Queering this card means looking at who in our community is comfortable, confident, and doing it all. If you're looking for a friend or mentor, this card is telling you to look for the person whose career is going well, who is always wrapped up in a million art or activist projects, and who is still always in their favorite queer spaces socializing easily and making connections. This card represents the drag moms in our community, but it represents the bar managers and owners, too. So often, queer or gay bars become our homes before we're able to make our own, and the person providing that home sits confidently on this card. If you are sober or bars are too overstimulating for you to hang out in safely, you could be led to a nearby coffee shop or drop-in center that you didn't even know was there until you started looking. This Queen is also any close friend you have that you look up to, quite frankly, for being confident in their queerness and owning the room when they walk into it. Maybe you need to be taken under their wing, but it's also possible you're being told to channel some of that energy yourself.

The Queen of Pentacles has already built the things she has in her life. Maybe you're being told as a queer person that now you get to rest, enjoy, and trust. There comes a point when we don't need to build anymore. We have fulfilled our purpose. We have created space in our communities for those who need it, our home lives are solid, and our careers are not going to take any more major hits. For queer people who have spent much of their life being shut down and marginalized, this time that should be easy and free can cause panic. We get into a mind-set where we feel like we need to be doing something and overcoming something all the time. That's exhausting, but it's all we know. This Queen does promise a better time, though, and your job is to enjoy the gifts, karma, and successes that come to you now—even if, as a traumatized or marginalized person, that's the hardest advice of all to take.

THE KING OF PENTACLES

The King of Pentacles has all of the success and sunny times ahead as this suit's Queen, but there are some key differences. The King has probably been a little more generous with his money or resources, but a little less open with his home or his heart. He has probably endured harsh obstacles to get where he is and isn't quite as able to let go of those memories as the Queen. If the Queen of Pentacles represents having it all, the King represents sacrificing intimacy and openness in order to get ahead. Now, though, things are different. By luck, design, or manifestation, the King shows a time in our life when the people in it are good and our life's situation is even better. This King does show up when we're considering moving or taking a big step forward in our career, but it also absolutely shows up when we need to reconsider our own work-life balance or be a little more open.

As a queer person, I have always related a lot to this King, in spite of the substantial differences between his presumed social class and mine. To get ahead in my careers and still be the activist I want to be, I have often sacrificed relationships and generosity of spirit to keep moving forward elsewhere. My support system is solid, but it is small, and as of writing this I am still romantically single as a result of being unwilling or unable to get out of hyper-motivated or hyper-community-oriented headspaces. Yet I have been generous, countless times, with my time, energy, and wallet (when able). The King of Pentacles as an energy sneaks up on us then, as queer people. We think we're doing the right things and moving our life the way we want it to go—and we are! And that's great! Then, one day we look around and the personal things we thought would fall into place haven't. We ended up in a nice house that does not feel like home, or still single, or without any real emotional connection to our community. This King is a call to really connect with the queer community you're already working for, to enjoy all of the sensuality life has to offer, and to remember that self-discipline is necessary sometimes to thrive as a queer person but the isolation that comes from nonstop work can be brutal. You deserve more than that if you are this King. You work so hard for queer or marginalized people to find equity while also carving out your space in your career field. Don't then punish yourself for succeeding by cutting off the emotion that makes life worth living.

Alternatively, as LGBTQQIP2SA+ people, the King of Pentacles sometimes shows up as a brilliant sign to take huge leaps of faith where activism or career is concerned. I've talked ad nauseum by now about the confidence hits that queer people take growing up in the world we live in. There are all kinds of growth and so many ways to get there, and this King can absolutely show up to promise that you not only have the resources, skills, and experience to make a huge leap, but also that your confidence level has soared high enough, too. I love when clients get this card as a manifestation of their confidence and what they can achieve, especially when those clients are marginalized people or have been deeply hurt and set back in their lives. It is now your time to dream big and achieve bigger, and when you've been as down and out as I know some of us have been, there isn't a better card to get to ease you into your next phase.

THE PAGE OF CUPS

This watery, emotion-driven suit gives us a Page that promises creative inspiration and new beginnings. If you're an artist, hope for this card when you're battling writer's block (or whatever your medium's form of that is), as it brings a lot of ideas and the ability to translate them to our work. For those who are not artists or creatives in the traditional way, this Page promises a unique way out of current problems and that thinking outside the box will pay off in your current endeavors. Connections with people new to your life are well aspected, and that includes a potential new romance! The youthful nature of this card promises the kind of relationships or friendships where you'll lose a whole day gallivanting through town together and spend many long nights giggling up a storm. As an energy, it is a time in your life where everything feels new and fresh—a phase where you're falling in love with life itself again, or perhaps with yourself for the first time. We also see in the Page of Cups a card that promises simple healing. As we go deeper into it, we see a recognition of the healing process we undertook in the numbered Cups cards. We are so well healed that we are new, and it's time to love like a new person.

There are very straightforward messages in the Page of Cups that translate easily for queer clients. That promise of new love can absolutely be true for us in this card. Particularly for polyamorous people who are interested in bringing on a new partner, this card bodes well. As a form of creative inspiration, those of us who are queer artists frequently struggle to find a balance between purely didactic work and something so expressing of ourselves that any kind of universal message gets convoluted. The Page of Cups is a good sign you are creating work that has a universally applied message and also speaks truly to your own experiences and vision as an artist. While I don't have statistics or numbers for this, there are a very large number of LGBTQQIP2SA+

artists primarily interested in telling their own stories or telling stories for specifically queer audiences. This card promises the inspiration or project you need to do that.

I rarely assign genders to the Pages, though if I do, it is a non-binary gender. This is particularly true of the Page of Cups. Traditional images see someone who is *maybe* young, but who is also, perhaps, going for an androgynous look that appeals to multiple genders. I see actual genderqueer friends of mine in quite a few depictions of the Page of Cups, so maybe that's where this interpretation comes from. Nonetheless, if someone I am reading for is asking about their own gender, this card is likely a sign that they are genderqueer or non-binary. The romantic side of this card promises that they will find love no matter how they present, but this card does encourage vulnerability and honesty in every area of our life.

When this card comes up, LGBTQQIP2SA+ people can be assured that they're entering a time where it's safe to be optimistic and hopeful. Youthful attitudes and even naivety pay off here. If you've been carrying around the burdens of being queer and letting that affect your mood, your heart, or your self-esteem, then this card is about turning a corner and no longer feeling the need to carry that burden. This Page loves love, and while that's a great aspiration, many of us become jaded thanks to bad experiences, being overwhelmed by life, or because of the callousness of the world around us. This is a card of hope and newness for everyone. For people who have been damaged and jaded because of a marginalized identity, it's also a promise that rest and peace are attainable and that they're coming your way.

THE KNIGHT OF CUPS

The Knight of Cups is one of the cards I relate most to in the whole tarot deck. This Knight fights for everything present in the Cups suit, namely emotional healing, love, and creative pursuits. This card does have a seductive side, though, and while that's often painted in a bad light, there is no harm in safe and consensual seduction of the people, experiences, or things you desire. This Knight is *not* trying to break hearts. If anything, they're trying to nurture and heal them (almost following the old campground guideline of "leave things better than you found them"). This Knight

just wants to love and to occasionally have that love returned to them. This means other people, sure. It also means coming to terms with themselves and falling in self-love. It means creating art that people love. It means finding romance and beauty in everything from a morning sunrise over Pisgah Forest to a pile of trash in their alleyway. While this Knight is definitively a lover and not a fighter, they will fight if someone or something they love is being threatened. They will also fight *for* love. This card is the artist who applies for twenty-five grants to fund a project they really believe in. This card is the partner who messes up but will do absolutely anything to make it up to you. This card is the best friend who will not let you forget your place in each other's lives.

Of course, there are good and bad sides to that. This Knight can come across as clingy. All of that water energy means they're sensitive to a fault and may use their fighting Knight's energy to lash out if they feel cornered. Because they will fight for art for art's sake, they can have their head completely in the clouds, unable to face reality or make ends meet financially. They usually make it big eventually, but it's a struggle to get there, and there was likely an easier way. Nonetheless, everybody loves the Knight of Cups as a collaborator, a partner, or friend. Their sobbing fits and disconnection from reality seem worth it when you look at the bounty of love and support they're constantly providing for you and their other loved ones.

Traditionally male, this is another court card I have always seen as genderqueer. Maybe it's because of the way I relate to it within my own gender fluidity, and maybe it's because I have several decks where a gender really can't be assumed unless you're looking for one. This means two things from a queer perspective. One is that this card *can be* any gender, and there may even be some gender fluidity involved with that. That also means, though, if your questions lie around your sexual identity, there is most likely fluidity there too. If you're asking whom you may end up with, this card disregards the gender of your future partner, keeping you wide open to all possibilities. If you're wondering if this person is the one for you even though you've always identified a different way, they likely are. It's a card that can indicate time to grow and explore and stretch into who you're meant to be, gender and sexuality wise. This Knight comes up a lot for partners of transgender people who are transitioning (or have recently transitioned). In spite of what that partner may have imagined about their own capacity for love, this card is assurance that it can be transcended. In fact, if you are trans and aren't sure how your partner is reacting, the Knight of Cups promises that your partner is on your side no matter what.

I connect so strongly to the Knight of Cups that queering it is actually difficult, because I have trouble finding things that *aren't* queer about this card. To me this Knight screams of the butch woman who wants to sweep me off my feet, of my own queer, masculine need to rush in and save my friends when they're in a bad situation, of all of the queer artists I've had the distinct pleasure to work with over the past several years who give and give and give to their art no matter how long it takes it to pay off. Finding something to queer beyond this card's very meaning is baffling to me. There aren't many cards that I stutter over when they come up for straight and cisgender people, but this is one of them. For queer seekers, then, this card begs you to go deep inside to your dreamiest, most romantic self and fight for the life you envision as that person. That is your best life. That is your best self. That is what this Knight wants you to fight for.

THE QUEEN OF CUPS

The Queen of Cups traditionally sits peacefully on her throne, looking a little bit dreamy. Dreamy as she is, though, she also has her feet firmly planted on the ground. This is someone who knows when to keep their emotions under wraps, and who is learning how to wield them powerfully without losing their cool. This Queen is intuitive, too. You're not going to get much by her, although, as a sensitive water sign they may bend their rules a little bit anyway. This Queen of Cups is compassionate and wants everyone in their kingdom to be happy and well fed. This is a confident Queen, and while they may be primarily concerned with providing for others, don't forget whose kingdom you're in. This Queen loves deeply and gives freely, but they are not a pushover.

Deeper interpretations of this card promise that if we are recovering from mental or emotional trauma, we are well on our way to healing and being in control of our emotions. That means things in our external lives are now becoming calm and secure, and this positively affects our internal lives. We can develop and nurture healthy relationships with our emotions and not worry about spiraling out of control if we give our sadness or anger the space it sometimes requires. This card, then, shows huge emotional growth. Our emotions aren't controlling us anymore. That means we can trust our intuition and trust that the things our own heart's desire are good for us again. This card has come up several times in my life, usually a couple of months after a breakthrough in therapy. This Queen is one I am always aspiring to reach, and that does give it an aspirational feel when it comes up in readings too.

Because the card is so much about being in control of your emotions and wielding them powerfully, I usually see this card as the head of the Cups suit, not the

King. If Cups by nature are emotional and sensitive, I have trouble believing that the card representing the peak of those traits has enough self-control in the face of their emotions to lead a kingdom. That makes our calm, collected, deeply intuitive Queen our leader, and that is leadership we can all agree we need.

Queer seekers will also find this card reassuring, although it is a little bit different for us. Being somewhere where it's safe to be ourselves and explore our emotions doesn't just have emotional meaning. It usually means that our employer is pro-queer, our roommate is a good ally that just wants us to feel safe, or that we are building a life that allows us to heal and move on from our past. Maybe we have even pulled ourselves out of tough financial times and get to dig in and do some healing. This Queen could mean our therapy is working, our friendships are solid, and we're (gasp) happy in our relationship(s). For queer people she doesn't just bring stability, she brings healing.

This Queen is so deeply intuitive, but the number one thing that screws up the ability of my LGBTQQIP2SA+ clients and friends to understanding their intuition is the years we spent second-guessing ourselves and questioning our very identities. No matter how intuitive you are, if you're shoving it down because of harmful (or even just confusing) messages from everyone from your parents to television commercials, you're going to stop thinking you're intuitive. You're going to stop believing your third eye or your gut. You're going to question everything: who you are, whom you love, even what you see as right and wrong. Over time, we stop getting intuitive messages. I don't blame our intuitions for this (certainly if I keep getting talked over in a conversation, I'm going to stop talking), but it's not our fault either. This Queen of Cups showing up promises that your intuition is back, thanks to all of the brilliant healing work you've been doing. Not only is it back, but it's also better than ever and ready to guide you through your next steps. If you take nothing else away from the Queen of Cups in a reading, take this: your intuitive self is strong, beautiful, and true. Listen to her.

THE KING OF CUPS

The Kings are often considered the pinnacle of everything a suit represents; I don't actually follow that guideline for every suit, but this King stands out to me as containing the best and worst of the Cups. In the negative, that means being highly sensitive is likely closer to sensitive to a fault. Being emotional probably means intense mood swings followed by profound periods of feeling deep love and gratitude for everything around them.

This King is as deeply intuitive as the Queen, but may not be able to put up psychic guards as easily. In the positive, there is nothing that can make you feel as loved and supported as a King of Cups running up to you and wrapping you up in a big, earnest bear hug. These Kings are deeply generous, offering the literal shirt off their back to homeless people or even friends who blurt out, "Whoa, cool shirt." They're primarily generous of emotion and spirit, though. If you ask for a moment of their time or a shoulder to cry on, you've got it. If you give them your heart, you can feel assured that you already have theirs. They're breathtaking individuals, and as an energy you can bet you'll see gifts from your Divine, generosity from total strangers, and a deep need in yourself to give back.

While the King is often seen as being super balanced and in control emotionally, it is always their feelings and generosity that stand out to most of the readers I know. While the Queen promises balance is coming or that we have balance, the King's message is more about learning *to* balance. Whether it's your emotions, your relationships, or your creative life, something is getting more of your attention than it should be right now. This card says to rein it in. Develop some tools for your self-care tool kit that help you center yourself emotionally. You should also be prepared to rebalance your scales. If your love life is good but absorbing your life, it may be time to refocus on your creative and spiritual life. If you've spent weeks alone in your apartment painting, it may be time to tend to your relationships.

This card's message, that it's time to balance, speaks volumes to polyamorous querents. Sometimes this card shows up when you're trying to balance too many partners, or when parts of your emotional needs aren't being met because you're not balancing enough of them. The message could be to figure out how to nurture those needs yourself, but if you're not a monogamous person, you may need new emotional and romantic connections in your life. The Cups are all about love, so it is really important to prioritize that when this card comes up.

Balance in our love lives isn't just an important message for polyam LGBTQQ-IP2SA+ querents, though. This King has so much love to give that they may not realize they're not having their needs met until it's too late. Now they're wrung out and exhausted, and likely not willing to let you back into their lives or heart. Is it just queer lovers that make the mistake of overgiving? No, but it is a lot more common. Romance is woefully misrepresented in queer media, even above and beyond what it is in regular media. Love is so different than we think, and when you are working with dating less than 5 percent of the population, you are more likely to put more stock in your relationship, even when it's clear you're not on the same page. This King urges you to back off a little and take your relationship(s) more slowly. Romance is amazing but it can and often should happen slowly and over time. This King tells LGBTQQIP2SA+ people not to rush into things, and promises that if you take that advice, you can have everything you want.

This King, like the rest of the Cups, is also profoundly creative. Sometimes, though, they show up to provide straightforward advice when queer creatives are feeling stuck. Maybe you're not taking in enough art by LGBTQQIP2SA+ people, and are therefore feeling disconnected from the art or media you *are* seeing. This could be a simple message to get to a queer art exhibit near you or at least rewatch your favorite guilty pleasure gay TV show. It used to be crushingly hard to find such things. One of the great joys of living in the world of Netflix, Hulu, and Twitter is that your new queer crush may be just a few clicks away. Use the tools you have; the whole point of deconstructing tarot is to bring it into our everyday, modern lives. You never know what will unblock you creatively, and this King brings that super-fast message.

Alternatively, though, so many of our courts represent callings. Maybe there really isn't queer art where you are. Maybe there really isn't easy enough Internet access to find that entertainment. What can you innovate for yourself and your community? What can you create? This King promises us that you've got more than enough talent to develop something that blends your queerness with your skill set. So get cooking!

FINAL THOUGHTS ON QUEERING THE TAROT

When the opportunity to turn *Queering the Tarot* into a book came up, I was terrified. This is how I approach most good things that happen in my life: with abject terror. Yet as I wrote out the cards that hadn't been written yet, I felt this project take on a life of its own. I could feel my cards working through me more deeply and more significantly than I ever had before. As I went back and rewrote the Major Arcana I felt a huge shift in my own spiritual life. I felt more connected to you—to readers that I don't even know—as deeply as I did to close friends in my waking life. I tried to honor that connection with you every step of the way; I hope you could feel it too.

Through writing this book, tarot has, once again, saved, changed, and altered my life for the better. Yet that's not enough for me anymore. I'm not struggling to scrape by and survive like I once was. I'm not still searching for who I am, and I don't need to be saved.

Now, this project is about you. This project is about that ultimate goal that I originally had: helping other people save their own lives the way tarot helped me save mine. This is why, even in troubling political times, I encourage marginalized clients to look to the Cups cards that are full of love and laughter. This is why a Wands card can help you find your purpose. This is why a Swords card wants you to heal from your trauma or mental illness. This is why the Earth cards want you to grow. We as marginalized people are entitled to all of the laughter and love and healing and fire and growth that we have always deserved. Even now. Especially now.

Moving forward, my hope is that you will continue to question institutions. I hope you will continue to queer everything. I really, really hope you continue to trust the tarot. Most of all, I hope you continue to trust yourself. You are where the intuition and the magick lie. The tarot is a brilliant tool for tapping into that and allowing you to come fully into your own, but at some point none of this is about the tarot. At some point, like everything, it's about you. Allow this book, your deck of cards, and all of that strong and powerful magick you have inside yourself to help you go forward and burn down the doors you can't open. Or create new doors meant just for you. Or decide that a world with doors isn't for you. Create a whole new world, then, and know you did it your way.

Thank you, readers, for coming on this journey with me. Now, like The Fool, it's time to begin your own journey.

ACKNOWLEDGMENTS

This book has been a dream of mine for so long, and its ability to come to fruition was never going to be mine alone. It was always going to be a full, solid team and I want to first acknowledge how wonderful and supportive Weiser Books has been through this whole process. I especially want to thank Kathryn Sky-Peck for encouraging this project, working her butt off, and ultimately making this dream happen for me. The Weiser dream team also includes Jane Hagaman, Bonni Hamilton, and Eryn Eaton as well as a ton of other wonderful people who helped shape and make this book what it is. People that are brilliant writers, editors, marketers, and so much more: thank you, thank you, thank you.

I want to thank Robin Scott of *Urban Tarot* for making such a provocative and stunning deck and her publisher for letting us use it for this project.

I want to thank Kate and Taylor for pushing me to do this when I wasn't sure my writing was publishable in this format. Life is weird and it goes in weird ways but this book did happen in part because of your faith in it and me, and for that I'll always be grateful.

I want to thank Andy Birkey of The Column for taking a chance on an aspiring arts journalist and turning me into a proper writer. Similarly, and obviously, I want to thank Beth Maiden of Little Red Tarot for taking my early ideas and allowing me to turn them into something real and important. I also want to thank Beth for the beautiful foreword, and for being so supportive of my careers in a million different ways.

To my Eye of Horus family, especially Thraicie, "thank you" is not enough for the million acts of support, kindness, and dedication you've shown to me for the past several years, and I'm so thrilled to add a unique book to your shelves.

To my friends and family, especially my dad, my siblings, Abbie and BethAnne and Troy: your love and support are the primary reason I was able to finish this manuscript even in the height of a TBI, and I love you all so, so much for reasons far beyond that.

Finally, thank you seems like such a silly thing to say to someone who makes sure you eat, who loves you at your worst, who drives you all around the cities regardless of your whims, and who listens to you cry in frustration over something as simple as a phrase that won't turn. Acknowledgments seem so formal when you're building a life together. Still, if anyone in the world deserves to be acknowledged and thanked and loved here, it is Manny.

ABOUT THE AUTHOR

Cassandra Snow is a professional tarot card reader who teaches Queering the Tarot and Tarot for Beginners classes and coaches new and intermediate readers. Cassandra (she/they) is a writer and theatre maker in Minneapolis, Minnesota, one of two artistic directors of Gadfly Theatre Productions, a queer and feminist theatre company. Her work is focused on healing, empowerment, and liberation individually and collectively. In her free time she consumes excessive amounts of coffee, reads voraciously, and hikes when Minnesota weather and her rheumatoid arthritis allow. You can find more about her tarot practice at *www.cassandra-snow.com*.